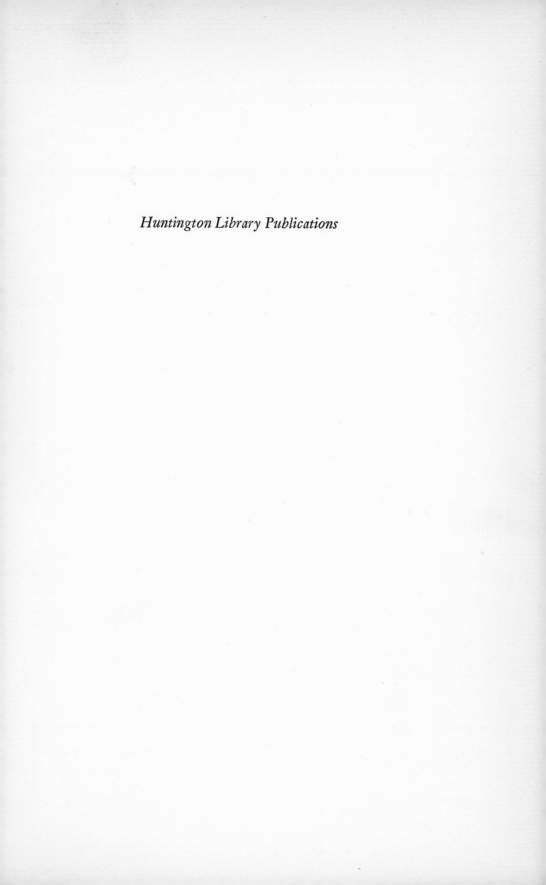

*Huntington Library Publications*

PORTRAIT OF DAVIS BY AN UNKNOWN ARTIST, PAINTED IN 1850

# AN AMERICAN IN CALIFORNIA

~ THE BIOGRAPHY OF
WILLIAM HEATH DAVIS
1822-1909

By Andrew F. Rolle

Henry E. Huntington Library

SAN MARINO, CALIFORNIA · 1956

PRINTED IN U.S.A. BY
ANDERSON, RITCHIE & SIMON : LOS ANGELES
DESIGN BY JOSEPH SIMON

TO ROBERT GLASS CLELAND

AND JOHN WALTON CAUGHEY

———————————————————

TWO WHO ENCOURAGED

# PREFACE

WILLIAM HEATH DAVIS was a pioneer of pioneers. During his long lifetime he saw the establishment of American institutions not only in California, but also in Alaska and Hawaii. In describing his role in this process Davis might appropriately have borrowed the words which Tennyson ascribed to Ulysses: "Much have I seen and known . . . I am a part of all that I have met."

Although Davis was not a dominant figure in world or national history, a study of his life reveals the heart of a past epoch. The activities of such a man often reflect the essence of a period more faithfully than does the story of more distinguished national figures. I have endeavored to let this study mirror the diversified times in which Davis lived.

His memory of the events through which he lived was phenomenal and he spent many of the autumn years of his life assembling these recollections into various lengthy manuscripts. Almost twenty years after his death his children brought hundreds of manuscript fragments to the San Francisco bookseller and occasional publisher, John Howell, who sorted and published them under the title, *Seventy-Five Years In California*. The New York *Times* called it "the best book of its kind about California. . . . as a mine of interesting, amusing, and romantic pictures of early California, the book is incomparable." And the work is just that—but it is not a biography of Davis nor does it cover more than a few decades of his career.

Because his published writings omit important aspects of his life, especially after 1850, I have sought to present the fuller biographical study which Davis himself did not complete. It is from the thousands of manuscripts that comprise his correspondence and unpublished writings that one gains a clearer and more intimate understanding of social, political, and economic conditions in California and the Pacific areas. These writings span the period from California's pastoral era to the threshold of the present. Davis and his early contemporaries have received relatively little attention by western writers, yet their story forms a significant chapter in the history of the Far West.

During the years of research and writing which this volume

vii

required I have become indebted to many individuals and institutions from Hawaii to Massachusetts. Some are listed in the Bibliography of Manuscripts which also indicates the location of the many manuscript collections on which this work is based. Though the list of persons who have been helpful is far too long to permit naming them individually, I cannot omit acknowledgment of the valuable criticism given this book at an earlier stage by Dr. John Walton Caughey and Dr. Roland D. Hussey of the University of California, Los Angeles. Again, at a date closer to final publication, both Dr. Caughey and his wife La Ree provided expert advice and stimulation. Dr. Lawrence Clark Powell, librarian and bookman, also gave sustained encouragement. At the Henry E. Huntington Library, Dr. Robert Glass Cleland has through the years characteristically and unfailingly reflected his own special brand of kindness.

To the Henry E. Huntington Library and its Trustees go my thanks for an invaluable Rockefeller grant-in-residence that materially aided the completion of the present volume. Dean Glenn S. Dumke and Dr. Raymond E. Lindgren, my colleagues at Occidental College, have been inordinately patient and helpful. The following people at one time or another either made documents available or gave valuable counsel: Dr. Andrew Horn, Librarian, University of North Carolina; Mr. James Mink of the Library of the University of California, Los Angeles; Miss Caroline Wenzel, California State Library; the late Dr. Cecil Corwin, Hayward, California; the late Mr. William Heath Davis King, Honolulu, Hawaii; Mr. Harry F. Bruning, Palto Alto; Miss Adele Ogden, Bancroft Library; Messrs. John and Warren Howell, San Francisco; Mrs. Alice Davis Riecker, Los Angeles; Mr. Jack Pollman, Los Angeles; Mrs. A. W. McCallum, San Diego; Dr. Edgeley W. Todd, Colorado Agricultural and Mechanical College; Dr. Edwin Carpenter, and Miss Mary Isabel Fry, Henry E. Huntington Library.

Like my obligation to the world of historical letters, the encouragement and aid given by my wife, Frances, cannot be repaid by the written word.

ANDREW F. ROLLE
OCCIDENTAL COLLEGE

# CONTENTS

# ILLUSTRATIONS

# Table of Abbreviations Used in Footnotes

BL: Bancroft Library, University of California, Berkeley, California.

HC: John Howell Collection, San Francisco, California.

LP: Thomas Oliver Larkin Manuscripts, Bancroft Library, University of California, Berkeley, California.

PPL: Letters, San Diego Pioneers, 1850-1855, Pasadena Public Library, Pasadena, California.

SL: William Heath Davis Collection, California State Library, Sacramento, California.

SLB: Spear Letter Book, Bancroft Library, University of California, Berkeley, California.

UCLA: William Heath Davis Collection, University of California Library, Los Angeles, California.

# AN AMERICAN IN CALIFORNIA

—

O F THE AMERICANS who came to California before the Gold Rush, William Heath Davis was one of the most influential and important. He belonged to that generation of pioneer Yankees who helped determine the province's economic and political future and who long antedated the first of the overland settlers.

Like his father before him Davis was only a boy when he made his first voyage into the Pacific. A few years later he began his trading career under a wise and experienced uncle, one of San Francisco's earliest merchants. Blessed by this trading background and training, Davis rapidly built up both a reputation and a fortune. His marriage into an important local family added materially to his position in California society and made him an adopted member of the native, landed aristocracy. For many years he was also in close association with the provincial officials, rancheros, and most important traders.

In his younger years Davis participated in the hide and tallow trade and lived through California's conquest and Gold Rush eras. Later he attained distinction as a merchant, town founder and developer, civic official, ship owner, ranchero, and even as an author. He witnessed the transformation of a vast and primitive frontier into the first stage of the society which is familiar to us today and became the patriarch of all the California pioneers.

For years he devoted himself to setting down elaborate recollections which he called the "Great Manuscript." In that narrative he paid homage to several generations of his forefathers. They were of a breed known in early nautical accounts as "Those Solid Men of Boston" and their deeds, whether in New England,

3

at Canton, or in Hawaii, Davis considered well worth recording. They were as vital to him as his own trading years before the mast and on horseback in California. These men were part of the story which he wrote near the end of his life and which the great San Francisco earthquake kept him from telling in full.

From his ancestors Davis acquired the sense of duty and frugality typical of early New Englanders. The Heaths, Holmeses, and Davises from whom he was descended were well-known families at the time of the American Revolution. The first Heaths had come from England in the seventeenth century to take up lands in a "state of nature" near Roxbury, Massachusetts, where Davis's most illustrious forebear, General William Heath, was born. This great-grandfather, the last surviving major general of the Revolution, enjoyed a close relationship with George Washington[1] and inspired three generations of Davises to use Heath as a middle name.[2]

Davis's paternal grandfather, "General" Robert Davis, participated in the Boston Tea Party and was the first of the family to enter the field of trading. His grandson brought this tradition to full attainment in waters far removed from Boston.[3]

There was also a mercantile background on his mother's side of the family. In 1791 his maternal grandfather, Oliver Holmes, first shipped from Boston around Cape Horn into the Pacific. The *Margaret*, on which he sailed, was among the earliest ships to engage in the trade between New England, the Northwest American coast, and China. This trafficking involved bartering cheap New England products such as jew's harps, mirrors, nails, and scrap iron for the valuable furs of sea otter and seal collected by the northwest Indians.

On this trip the *Margaret* touched at the Sandwich Islands and

[1]See "Heath Papers," *Collections* of the Mass. Hist. Soc., 5th Ser. (Boston, 1878), IV, 1-28, later reprinted as *Memoirs of Major General William Heath By Himself*, ed. William Abbatt (New York, 1901), p. 1.

[2]There were living during the 1950's an Oliver Holmes King, a William Heath Davis King, a William Heath Davis King, Jr., a Roy Heath Davis, and a William Heath Davis King III.

[3]For some little-known facts about Eliza Davis Dana, the daughter of "General" Robert Davis, and sister of William Heath Davis, Sr., see Helen S. Giffen, "An Adopted Californian: the Life and Letters of William Goodwin Dana," *Quarterly*, Hist. Soc. of S. Calif., XIX (1937), 62n.

Davis's grandfather, who had originally sailed for China, never reached the Orient. At his own request Holmes was permitted to remain on Oahu Island. Here other seamen were accustomed to stay from a month to a year, but Holmes remained the rest of his life, dying thirty-two years later in the village of Honolulu which he preferred to any place in New England.[4]

Holmes proved to be no ordinary citizen of the land of his adoption. Shortly after his arrival he met and married Mahi, a Polynesian princess, and he eventually served as Governor of Oahu for Hawaii's King, Kamehameha I. Next to the King he was considered "the greatest chief on the island."[5] He acquired plantations on various islands and also developed a sandalwood and ship chandlery business. Mahi bore him six children and provided him an orderly family life. Despite his wealth Holmes adhered to the customs of the country, even living in a grass hut. Guests at his banquets were often served roast dog by waiters wearing a livery consisting of "a cincture of country cloth round the waist from which a narrow piece of the same stuff passed between the legs and was fastened to the belt."[6]

The Hawaii to which Holmes came was a land of striking contrasts. The natives still lived on an abundance of tropical fruits, roots, and fish. Rich soil, heavy rainfall, and uniform temperatures made life easy. At about the time Holmes arrived,

[4]"Certificate of Honesty," Oct. 8, 1793, MS, property of the late W. H. D. King, Honolulu, Hawaii, indicates that Holmes took passage aboard the "P. W. Henry of N. Castle to Whahoo from Owyhee." Captain W. Wake, after whom Wake Island was named, executed a certificate that Holmes was not a deserter, dated Jan. 3, 1796; see also William Heath Davis, Seventy-Five Years in California; a history of events and life in California . . . , ed. Douglas S. Watson (San Francisco, 1929), p. 101. Hereafter cited as 75 Years.

[5]Harold Whitman Bradley, The American Frontier In Hawaii; the pioneers, 1789-1843 (Stanford, Calif., 1942), p. 38; Amasa Delano, A Narrative of Voyages and Travels, in the Northern and Southern hemispheres: comprising three voyages round the world . . . (Boston, 1817), p. 395.

[6]Victor S. K. Houston, "Madame de Freycinet in Hawaii, 1819," Paradise of the Pacific (Honolulu, Mar.-Apr. 1937), pp. 20 ff.; Ross Cox, Adventures On The Columbia River including the narrative of a residence of six years on the western side of the Rocky Mountains . . . together with a journey across the American continent (New York, 1832), pp. 38-41; Hiram Bingham, A Residence of Twenty-One Years In The Sandwich Islands, or the civil religious and political history of those islands: comprising a particular view of the missionary operations connected with the introduction and progress of Christianity and civilization among the Hawaiian people (New York, 1847), p. 103, pp. 105-106.

however, Hawaii's natives were being squeezed between two Yankee forces: on the one hand, were the boisterous foreign seamen who visited the islands; on the other, were Congregational missionaries called "Longnecks" by some. These ministers of the gospel found the natives' idolatry so weak that Hawaii provided them a fertile field of work. Inevitably the missionaries and seamen clashed.

In this conflict Holmes, who was trying to live a respectable life ashore, sided with the missionaries. Seamen, fresh from Arctic waters, not only came into conflict with them, but also with Holmes—especially when they insisted on taking native girls aboard their ships. An early maritime journal once recorded that an American shipmaster fired upon Holmes with a pistol, while other members of his crew cursed and kicked the expatriate Yankee, "saying that they were Kings of this island." With the help of some natives, Holmes drove these offenders away.

Among the many seamen who came to Hawaii in that early day was a young, lean, and rawboned man named Captain Davis who became a favorite of Holmes and married his eldest daughter, Hannah. To them were born two sons, the younger of whom, William Heath Davis, Jr., is the subject of this biography. William's father, Captain Davis, emerged in time as an exploiter of the trans-Pacific sandalwood traffic, part of the China trade that developed into an almost legendary aspect of American commerce. Because the Revolutionary War had deprived American merchants of the imperial trade preference they once enjoyed, such men were forced to seek new markets in the Pacific. This search for trade outlets led Captain Davis, as it did many of his contemporary New Englanders, both to Hawaii and to the docks of Canton, China.

At Hawaii William's father wove his family fortunes with those of the Pacific. Here Captain Davis and other mariners found a refuge, a depot for repairing both their ships and spirits, and a port for loading cargoes of sandalwood. He exchanged the fragrant wood, locally known as *iliahi*, in Canton for tea, china, silks, and nankeen.

Captain Davis first entered the China trade in 1807 when he cleared the vessel *Mercury* out of Boston. For more than ten

6

years the captain engaged in highly successful commercial operations including the China trade, business with the Russians in Alaska and off the California coastline, trade operations southwest of that Spanish province, and the very fruitful sandalwood trade between the Sandwich Islands and China.[7]

Captain Davis succeeded in tying his fortunes to those of his wife's birthplace, and like his father-in-law, was a prominent member of Honolulu's American community. His wealth grew and he at first had reasonably cordial relations with the missionaries. But he had no lasting affection for his religious neighbors and they soon forgot the charitable acts he had performed for them. When the captain engaged in trading which they considered unethical the missionaries were quick to voice their disapproval. Nor did they approve of his drinking which became more and more frequent as he grew older and during his later years, Captain Davis appeared often in the writings of Oahu's missionaries as a derisive figure. When the captain died in 1822 the missionaries regarded his death with a certain satisfaction.[8] One missionary, Elisha Loomis, wrote in his diary, "He literally killed himself with strong drink." But the missionaries may have preached too strongly about the sins of the deceased. This is implied in a lay diary which recorded that many Americans attending the funeral "were disgusted with the Sermon of the missionary about Captain Debes [Davis]."[9]

The captain's death left Hannah with her baby, William Heath

[7]The subject of William Heath Davis's father's career is too extensive to include in this biography. The sources for it are extremely widespread and varied. The Astor Papers, Hunnewell Papers, and Marshall Papers at the Harvard University Library, Cambridge, Mass., are especially replete with references to this early Pacific mariner. An indication of the excitement that characterized his career is to be found in Andrew F. Rolle, "The Eagle Is Seized," *Westways* XLVI (1954), 16-17.

[8]A basic source covering the last few years of Captain Davis's stormy life is the "Manuscript Journal of Elisha and Maria Loomis," in the possession of Miss Albertine Loomis, Detroit, Michigan. The thorny relationship between the competing mariners and missionaries at Hawaii deserves further attention. Albertine Loomis, *Grapes of Canaan* (New York, 1951) is the most recent unfavorable appraisal of Captain Davis's group. Louis B. Wright and Mary Isabel Fry, *Puritans in the South Seas* (New York, 1936) also treat the subject but reach different conclusions.

[9]See MS journal of the Andalusian Don Francisco de Paula Marin, "Journal 1809-1826," pp. 46-47 in Marin Collection, Archives of Hawaii, Honolulu, Hawaii.

Davis, Jr., born in 1822, and a three-year-old son, Robert. Although Hannah inherited her husband's island property, his will allocated her little else. Five thousand dollars, a large sum for that day, was given to each of the following New Englanders, who later played a part in the life of the captain's sons: Thomas Meek, John C. Jones, Jr., Eliab Grimes, and a nephew, William Goodwin Dana. Though in his will the captain made no mention whatever of his wife or his younger son and namesake, he expressed the hope that his son, Robert, would "never forget those ties which bind him to the mother who gave him birth."[10] Mystery surrounds the attitude of Hannah and her children toward the deceased captain, for following his death she returned to the use of her maiden name. Only William later made an effort to keep the captain's memory alive.[11]

About 1826 William's mother, Hannah, married John Coffin Jones who greatly influenced the boy's early years and future life. Jones was the most important American in Hawaii. In addition to his official position as United States Commercial Agent for the islands, he traded on his own and also represented numerous Boston shippers. The great distance of his post from the American capital, and the general debility of the monarchy, made it possible for this unusual man to play an extraordinary role in Hawaiian affairs.

During the period when Jones represented the United States, Hawaii was still a place where he and other merchants could do much as they pleased. Jones himself described the Honolulu of that early day as "one of the vilest places on the globe." Seamen from all nations crowded its score or more of grog shops and consorted with its women of easy virtue. Most of Honolulu's foreign residents were said to divide their time about equally between gambling, drinking, and sleeping.[12]

[10]This reference, as far as determinable, is to Hannah, the mother of both his children whom he may not have married in a Christian ceremony. A copy of Captain Davis's will, dated Jan. 23, 1822, is in this writer's possession through the courtesy of Mrs. Helen Giffen of San Francisco.

[11]William Heath Davis, "Glimpses of the Past," p. 1, Bancroft Library MS. Hereafter cited as "Glimpses."

[12]Bradley, *American Frontier*, pp. 83, 89.

Robert lived in this environment, so wicked by New England standards, until he was five, when his stepfather sent him to Massachusetts to be educated in a "classical manner." William, however, remained in the islands and went to sea before he reached his teens. William's formative years, therefore, were bound up with the sea and with the village of grass shacks which was Honolulu. Yet from this environment he absorbed but little of the coarseness that had marred his father's character.

In 1831, when he was only nine years old, William made his first trip to Alaska and California, sailing with his stepfather aboard the *Louisa*, one of his eight trading vessels. In contrast to semi-tropical Honolulu, gales greeted the *Louisa* in the North Pacific and the waves rose almost high enough to justify the saying that sailing vessels occasionally emerged from Arctic storms with seaweed clinging to their yardarms.

Upon arrival at Sitka, which he feared he would never reach, the boy found much to please his fancy. The fortified Russian towers, against which the wind lashed, stimulated his imagination. He watched with interest while Jones bartered Boston goods for sea otter furs and strange currency. Here William was being introduced to the trade his father had pioneered during the opening years of the century. He took a boy's delight in the festivities at the fort to which he and his stepfather were invited and in the reciprocal entertainments held on board the *Louisa*. Young as he was, William was charmed by Sitka's Russian ladies of the better class who had come thousands of miles from their homeland to an outpost in Alaska. Long afterwards he remembered them as "delicate and symmetrical in form and figure, and exceedingly graceful in their walk and carriage."

After completing trading operations in Russian America, Jones sailed the *Louisa* southward. In California, because of Mexico's independence from Spain, a large number of American vessels regularly visited the province's "leeward ports" south of Monterey: Santa Barbara, San Pedro, and San Diego. In San Diego, the most southerly of California's harbors, the *Louisa* took on a deckload of hides and horses, both in short supply at Honolulu, and then set her course for the islands.[13] The voyage homeward followed a routine course and was uneventful, except that William broke his arm when he fell into an open hatch.

His first experience with ships and sails on this voyage made it hard for William to look forward with any pleasure to the humdrum prospect of school at Honolulu. Nevertheless his stepfather enrolled him among the first pupils of the Oahu Charity School, a recently founded missionary institution of which Jones was a trustee and which would eventually attract pupils from as far away as California.[14]

In 1833 Jones interrupted William's schooling, much to the latter's delight, to use his services as a cabin boy on a voyage to California. The two went to sea on the bark *Volunteer* of which Jones was owner and supercargo.[15] Upon arrival at Yerba Buena, young William could find only one person living at that forlorn landfall, later the site of San Francisco. At low tide this solitary resident tended a potato patch near the mud flats some distance from Mission Nuestra Señora de los Dolores. Though the mission had begun its period of long decline, it still dominated the peninsula's life. At the close of the Spanish period it grazed thousands of cattle, sheep, and horses, owned large numbers of hogs and oxen, and kept on hand great quantities of wheat. William, wholly unaccustomed to seeing such agricultural wealth in his native Hawaii, looked with amazement at the possessions of the

[13]*75 Years*, p. 206. A lively horse trade flourished between California and Hawaii from 1825-1840. L. H. Anthon to Davis, Feb. 24, July 15, 1840, William Heath Davis Collection, Calif. State Library, Sacramento, Calif. Hereafter cited as SL. This letter stated there were then no horse races in Hawaii for lack of horses.

[14]"Glimpses," p. 4; Bradley, *American Frontier*, pp. 382-84; Ralph S. Kuykendall, *The Hawaiian Kingdom, 1778-1854; foundation and transformation* (Honolulu, 1947), p. 363. Stephen Reynolds to Nathan Spear, June 24, 1835, Cowan Collection, University of California at Los Angeles. Hereafter cited as UCLA.

[15]At Santa Barbara Davis witnessed the marriage of Thomas Oliver Larkin, later American Consul at California's capital, Monterey, to Rachel Holmes, one of the ship's passengers. After Jones performed the ceremony, the *Volunteer* headed for Yerba Buena. See William Heath Davis, *Sixty Years in California; a history of events and life in California* ... (San Francisco, 1889), p. 11. Hereafter cited as *60 Years*; Reuben L. Underhill, *From Cowhides to Golden Fleece, a narrative of California, 1832-1858, based upon unpublished correspondence of Thomas Oliver Larkin, trader, developer, promoter, and only American consul* (Stanford, Calif., 1946), p. 10.

mission. Though a Catholic establishment, it traded most of its hides and tallow to the many Protestant Yankee skippers such as Jones who, in spite of the unwieldy customs regulations retained by Mexico after her independence from Spain, sailed their vessels into the great landlocked bay of San Francisco.

After this second cruise to California Davis found life at the Hawaiian school even more tedious than before. From time to time he was encouraged to continue his studies by his brother, Robert, now approaching maturity in Boston. In one of his letters Robert wrote that he was "highly gratified" to receive his first written message from William and commented that his younger brother's progress was as good "as though you had been in America." But Robert further counseled:

I would recommend too, not only a care over your studies, but also an attention to the formation of your character, in order that you may become a virtuous as well as a learned man. Your situation is surrounded by many temptations, and it will be your glory to meet and overcome them. As I am so far separated from our beloved mother, I hope that you will be to her all that I should wish to be, if I were at the Sandwich Islands.[16]

William, chiefly because of the insistence of his stepfather and brother, remained in school until 1838 when he was sixteen years old. In February of that year Jones wrote him from Santa Barbara and promised, "when I come back to Oahu, I will give you some goods and set you up in a store for yourself." This was probably the most exciting news that Davis had ever received. As long as he could remember he had wanted, above everything else, to become a trader. His stepfather clearly stressed, however, that William's future career depended upon his behavior. Jones warned the lad not to "keep with the boys who go with the King"; assured him that if he would look after "little Johnny and Elizabeth" (Jones's two children by Hannah), he would do everything possible for him; and closed with the admonition, "believe me when I tell you, that as long as you behave like a Gentleman I shall be your friend and protector."[17]

[16]R. G. Davis to Davis, Nov. 2, 1836, SL.
[17]Jones to Davis, Feb. 1, 1838, SL.

But instead of taking advantage of his stepfather's offer to set him up as a storekeeper in Honolulu, William quit his schooling in Hawaii and went to live with his uncle, Nathan Spear, a prosperous and influential merchant in California. Married to Jane Holmes, one of William's aunts, Spear had recently promised William that he would take him into his employ whenever the boy wanted to leave the islands.[18]

Perhaps William's abrupt departure from Hawaii occurred because of the following enigmatic item which was printed in the *Sandwich Island Gazette* of January 27, 1838:

Married on Friday evening, January 21st by Rev. Lowell Smith, Mr. William H. Davis to Kaimiaina.

This short newspaper notice which appeared just before he received his stepfather's letter is the only mention of a marriage by William with a native woman. He himself never referred to it in later years and no other allusion to it has been found. In some way as yet unexplained such an event could have caused Davis to make his permanent residence with his uncle in California.

Some years before the Californians knew the nature of a New England store, Spear had risked his meager finances to open a business at Monterey. He found that the goods which he imported from the Orient, Honolulu, and Boston were still in as much demand as when William's father had traded in California waters. In partnership with two other pioneers, Jacob P. Leese and William S. Hinckley, Spear eventually opened a second store at Yerba Buena and by the time Davis joined him, he was probably the best-known trader on San Francisco Bay.[19]

Before reaching Yerba Buena, Davis's ship stopped at Monterey. Here the lad saw much to arouse within him an affection for the California land that for the remainder of his life was to be his home. Monterey itself contained numerous whitewashed houses, very different both in architecture and attractiveness from the small mud-colored adobes found in most other California pueblos, and the red-tiled roofs offered a striking contrast to the forest of pines which rose above them. Monterey, long the residence of

[18]"Glimpses," p. 11.
[19]R. G. Davis to Davis, Nov. 16, 1839, SL.

the governor, was the first port of entry for all ships trading along the coast. Profiting socially from its official atmosphere, the capital was the most civilized place in California.

Upon this, his third visit to Monterey, Davis was the guest of Major William Warren, who then managed Nathan Spear's store at the capital. Warren's home afforded a place of entertainment for the supercargoes and captains of the many ships anchored in the harbor. In Warren's dining room Davis met a vanguard of the Americans soon to descend upon California. In addition to Thomas O. Larkin, with whom he was already acquainted, he also met many mariners, whalers, sealers, and traders. Their presence on this remote frontier indicated that foreigners were already filtering into California. Sooner than was suspected these Americans would exert an effect of the most revolutionary character upon Mexico's isolated and remote province.

Following his brief stay at Monterey Davis continued his voyage to Yerba Buena on the *Alert*, a vessel which Richard Henry Dana introduced to a worldwide audience in his *Two Years Before the Mast*. As the *Alert* sailed into San Francisco Bay the first building that Davis saw was his uncle's waterfront home, a conspicuous landmark called Kent Hall. Spear had constructed this residence from the superstructure of a ship which gave the house its name.

Although Mexican citizens could be granted public land by the government, as a foreigner, Spear could not legally obtain the ground on which his house and adjoining store were built without purchasing the property. Unlike many Americans in California, he refused to give up his citizenship in order to qualify for such a free cession by the governor. Instead he bought the land outright. As his nephew later explained, "Nathan Spear ... loved his country far above the temptation of a grant of eleven square leagues of the best land in the Department of California, which he could have had by denouncing his mother country to become a naturalized citizen of Mexico."[20]

In the household of such a man Davis found that the months

[20]75 *Years,* p. 137, pp. 174-75; Nathan Spear to John Perry, Apr. 20, 22, 1839, and Spear to Larkin, Apr. 22, 1839, "Spear Letter and Account Book," Bancroft Library MS. Hereafter cited as SLB.

passed as though they were weeks. Just a year after his arrival at Yerba Buena, the unloading of his uncle's long-awaited grist mill off a ship from Baltimore changed his daily routine of store tending. The appearance of this first mill in northern California caused a stir along the entire coast. Spear housed it in a frame building near his store and put four to six mules to work turning the arrastra-like mill. The whole structure shook incessantly when the machinery was in operation but Spear's mill ground twenty-five barrels of badly needed dark flour a day. Its owner, with Yankee ingenuity, turned the mill to other uses as well. The French explorer, Duflot de Mofras, when he visited Yerba Buena, commented enthusiastically on the ingenious tasks to which the mill's machinery had been adapted. Spear not only had a grist mill, but also a device to saw lumber, make shingles, turn a lathe, and run a bolting apparatus for refining flour.[21]

The new mill met with such success that Davis's uncle was obliged to hire a miller, a cooper, and a man who served as both butcher and cook. This freed his nephew, in whose ability and judgment Spear placed increasing confidence, to go far afield on horseback to advertise the mill's many services and to seek customers for its products. In addition to the journeys they made on horseback, Davis and Spear used a number of launches to reach rancheros who lived near the headwaters of the Sacramento and San Joaquin rivers. William usually operated a boat named the *Isabel* to convey grain from distant ranchos to the mill and to carry back cargoes of flour. On such trips he also arranged to buy cattle, hides, and tallow from the rancheros.

Grain production in northern California was larger at that time than most writers on the period are aware, and from such ranchos as that of General Mariano Guadalupe Vallejo, military commander of northern California, Davis sometimes obtained as much as five or six hundred *fanegas*—between thirty-five and forty tons—of wheat to be ground into flour at Spear's mill. Gen-

[21]Hubert Howe Bancroft, *History of California* (San Francisco, 1890), III, 103; IV, 667-68n; Eugène Duflot de Mofras, *Duflot de Mofras' Travels on the Pacific Coast . . .* trans., ed., and annot. by Marguerite Eyer Wilbur (Santa Ana, 1937), I, 227-28; Zoeth S. Eldredge, *Beginnings of San Francisco from the expedition of Anza, 1774, to the city charter of April 15, 1850* (San Francisco, 1912), II, 530-531.

14

eral Vallejo used the flour to feed both the government soldiers at Sonoma and the many Indians, servants, and laborers whom he maintained upon his two large ranchos. Davis also obtained orders from the northern California missions and the Russians at Fort Ross to grind their grain at his uncle's mill.[22]

Though the business of the mill kept him occupied, Davis usually held his Sundays free for hunting. On such occasions he and the miller flushed innumerable coveys of quail in the nearby fields and shot large numbers of deer in the scrub oaks and sprouting willow thickets along the shore of San Francisco Bay.

For many years—indeed until his wife drank of the supposedly miraculous waters of a nearby spring and bore him a son—Spear had no children of his own and came to look upon his nephew as a responsible substitute. As a member of his uncle's household at Yerba Buena, Davis performed his duties conscientiously, proved a valuable and trustworthy assistant to his older relation, and, though stubborn by nature, followed Spear's advice. In a day when apprentices often ran away from the employers to whom they were legally bound, Spear wrote to John Coffin Jones: "Wm. H. Davis is still with me! I believe he is satisfied and content; he is obedient and industrious. I think him a good boy, & he promises to become a good man."[23]

William soon had an opportunity to show his ability and initiative in an important capacity. One morning early in July 1839, a mixed company of Germans, Swiss, and Hawaiian adventurers led by the redoubtable emigrant, Captain Johann Augustus Sutter, arrived at Yerba Buena. Sutter would one day achieve a distinctive place in the history of California. Although called "a dreamer with a gifted tongue," he established a fort and a ranch that became a place of respite for scores of American immigrants who crossed the plains and who might have died of starvation were it not for Sutter's warmhearted hospitality. Ultimately it was at his sawmill on the American river that gold was discovered in California, an event that materially affected the history of the province.

[22]Spear to Alexander Rotcheff, Jan. 16, 1839, July 11, 1840, and to Victor Castro, May 22, 1840, SLB.
[23]Aug. 24, 1838, SLB.

Sutter had left Switzerland for the United States secretly five years before in order to escape a debtor's prison. He tarried briefly in the Mississippi Valley, visited parts of Mexico along the Santa Fe Trail, sailed to Honolulu and the Russian colony of Alaska, and finally appeared as a guest at Spear's establishment in Yerba Buena. Sutter already had a partly formulated plan of colonization and a dream of empire in his fertile, if not predictable, brain. He proposed to establish in California a self-sustaining colony of Americans, to be called New Helvetia, near the junction of the American and Sacramento rivers in a primitive area that he marked on a creased and well-worn map as the "Sacramento Val." Soon after his arrival in California Sutter visited Governor Alvarado at Monterey. He obtained official permission to settle on some 50,000 acres of land well upstream from the region in which Davis had been accustomed to trade. Except for the wanderings of occasional hunters and trappers the area had remained virtually unexplored.

When the Swiss requested Spear to provide him with supplies and a guide for the expedition up the Sacramento River to the site of his proposed trading post, Spear at once recommended Davis. Because his nephew was one of the few persons in Yerba Buena who had traveled into the interior recently, it was natural that he should be asked to convey Sutter toward that wilderness. Two launches, the *Isabel* and the *Nicholas*, were assigned to take Sutter's party of foreigners up the river. Though Sutter also brought along his own four-oared boat, Davis called the *Isabel*, which he commanded, the "flagship of the fleet."

Fearful of the Indians whom he expected to encounter in the Sacramento Valley, Sutter had equipped himself with two pieces of light artillery. When, after eight days, the company reached the vicinity of the future capital of California, they found some seven or eight hundred Indians awaiting their arrival. Sutter prepared his men to resist an attack, but the Indians were more curious than hostile and large numbers of them ventured out on the water to greet them in *tule balsas*, floats made of the fibrous rushes that grew on the river banks. Reassured by this friendly encounter, Sutter and his companions turned up the American River where it joined the Sacramento, landed at a convenient anchor-

16

age, and pitched their tents near the stream. Here a real enemy lay in wait for the invaders. Both Davis and Sutter reported that each evening myriads of vicious Sacramento mosquitoes attacked the members of their party.[24]

As soon as it became evident that Sutter and his men would survive the wilderness, Davis began his return trip down the Sacramento to Yerba Buena. As his two boats left the anchorage Sutter fired a salute in honor of his departing guide, an act that produced unexpected results. Before the noise of the cannon died away hundreds of Indians crowded into Sutter's camp and large numbers of deer and elk ran crazily out of the nearby woods. As Davis later described the scene, "the howls of wolves and coyotes filled the air, and immense flocks of water fowl flew wildly about over the camp."

Returning Sutter's salute with nine cheers, Davis and his companions headed down the river. Davis later called this farewell, "the first echo of civilization in the primitive wilderness," and took pride in the fact that he had conveyed the founder of Sacramento to the site on which he built a fort to rule for a few years as lord of an imperial domain.[25]

A long and damp trip downstream reduced Davis's small party to a diet of brown sugar and when their boats came to anchor near present-day Martinez they called the place, with some justice, the Valley of Hunger. A member of the group fortunately found and killed a steer, which restored their energies. When Davis finally reached Yerba Buena, Spear commended his nephew for the way in which he had handled the expedition. For both men it was a real satisfaction to have helped to establish a new settlement in the wilderness.

Soon after the Sacramento venture Davis learned that his stepfather had left Honolulu to become a resident of nearby Santa Barbara. There were a number of reasons for this unexpected

[24]*60 Years*, p. 17; Bancroft, *History*, III, 130-131; Johann Augustus Sutter, *Neu-Helvetien; Lebenserinnerungen des generals Johann Augustus Sutter* (Frauenfeld, Switzerland, 1944).

[25]"Glimpses," p. 14; of the many secondary accounts of Davis's role in the Sutter story, the fullest are James Peter Zollinger, *Sutter; The Man and His Empire* (New York, 1939), pp. 65, 117, and Julian Dana, *Sutter of California* (New York, 1938), pp. 76, 81, 82, 125, 378.

17

change of residence. Jones, like Captain Davis, cordially disliked the American missionaries in Hawaii. He believed that an alliance between them and the native chiefs would curtail the growing trade between the United States and the islands. He had repeatedly defied the missionary group and his opinionated dispatches about them were printed verbatim in official United States publications.[26] The missionary-influenced Hawaiian government had recently charged Jones with dereliction of duty, bigamy, tampering with the morals of the natives, and absence from his post. President Van Buren accordingly removed the New Englander from his position as American Commercial Agent at Honolulu.[27]

Weary of criticism by the missionaries, no longer in government employ, and tired of his wife, Jones left Honolulu. In Santa Barbara he became so enamored of Manuela Carrillo, daughter of California's sometime governor, that he abandoned all thought of returning to Hawaii and his wife and married the California señorita.[28] Hannah ultimately "divorced" Jones, but continued to live in his Honolulu coral house and retained the lands she inherited from William's father. For William such distant properties became the source of distracting litigation. As long as the family struggle with the missionaries continued, he received his mother's and brother's written complaints against the "infernal missionaries."[29] He was also frequently reminded by the family that island friends did not admire what they called William's "miserable place California."[30]

[26]U. S. Senate, "Report of the Secretary of the Navy," *Senate Exec. Doc. No. 1*, 21st Cong., 2nd Sess. (Washington, 1830), pp. 202-205; William S. W. Ruschenberger, *Narrative of a Voyage Round the World during the years 1835, 36, and 37* (London, 1938), II, 383-84.

[27]Stephen Reynolds to Spear, Nov. 14, 1839, Jan. 19, 1840, UCLA; Bradley, *American Frontier*, pp. 301-304.

[28]Isaiah Lewis to Davis, Jan. 26, 1840, SL; Gorman Gilman, "Streets of Honolulu In The Early Forties," *Thrum's Hawaiian Annual* (Honolulu, 1904), pp. 91-92; R. J. Baker, of Honolulu, to the author, Aug. 8, 1950.

[29]John C. Jones, Jr. to Davis, July 9, 1900, Howell Collection, San Francisco, hereafter cited as HC, states that "Emanuela," the writer's mother, died that year in Nice, France. See also George Nidever, *Life and Adventures of George Nidever*, ed. William Henry Ellison (Berkeley, 1937), p. 59.

[30]Alexander Galman to Davis, May 15, 1840, SL; Reynolds to Larkin, Jan. 21, 1840, and A. B. Thompson to Larkin, July 2, 1839, Larkin Papers, Bancroft Library. Hereafter cited as LP.

18

To be sure, disturbed political conditions in that province kept some foreigners in a state of uncertainty. This confusion was only a reflection of the near anarchy then prevalent in Mexico. In 1840 tensions between California's government and its foreign residents became especially acute when Governor Juan B. Alvarado issued an order for the arrest of certain suspicious foreigners reported to be plotting against his administration. The leader in the affair was said to be Isaac Graham, a hunter and trapper from Kentucky. Because of his distrust of such American frontiersmen, the governor ordered the arrest of Graham and some forty others in various places throughout the province.[31]

The governor placed Yerba Buena under martial law and sent a number of its foreign residents under guard to Monterey and then to Mexico. Both Davis and his uncle, who had little use for "mountain men" of Graham's type, were also placed under arrest for a short period. Though embarrassing this action was almost a formality, and while complying with the order to detain foreigners the sub-prefect of Yerba Buena showed his friendship for Davis by sending him to Mission Dolores which was temporarily used as a prison. During this twenty-four-hour period of confinement that official's thoughtful wife organized a dance for the prisoner out of regard for their past friendship. The popular Davis had such a fine time at this fandango that he devoted far more space to describing the evening's entertainment in his later writings than he did to his arrest. His uncle Nathan, who underwent a similar polite "imprisonment," was quickly released, as were various other reputable foreigners.[32]

Eventually those Americans who had been manhandled and

[31]Bancroft, *History*, IV, 10, states that Davis erred in describing the 1840 uprising in his "Glimpses," pp. 30-35. See also Thomas J. Farnham, *Travels in the Californias, and Scenes in the Pacific ocean* (New York, 1844).

[32]Among those not molested were J. B. R. Cooper, Abel Stearns, and Davis's cousin William Goodwin Dana. Spear and Larkin were the only two Americans in California allowed to live without the annoying restrictions applied to foreigners. Both held a governmental *carta de seguridad* and were permitted legal residence without adopting American citizenship. See *The Larkin Papers*, ed. George Peter Hammond (Berkeley, 1951-    ), I, ix and Underhill, *Cowhides*, p. 62; Bancroft, *History*, IV, 17; Robert Glass Cleland, *The Early Sentiment For the Annexation of California: an account of the growth of American interest in California from 1835 to 1846* (Austin, Texas, 1915), pp. 21-23.

taken to Mexico were given free passage home. The governor, furthermore, received instructions to accord Americans every assistance in regaining property lost during their arrest.[33]

In spite of the "Graham Affair" Davis could still write his brother Robert, who had returned to Hawaii, that he wanted to remain in California. Busily engaged in conducting his uncle's business, he refused a position as supercargo aboard the Ecuadorian brig *Joven Carolina*. He seemed to sense that the preparation of daily invoices, tending store, checking cargo lists, and keeping accounts current were but preliminaries to a fuller career of his own. His determination to succeed, added to the attractions of California, held him fast to the new land of his adoption.

[33]Concerning his desires for American protection by a warship such as "Old Ironsides," see Davis to R. G. Davis, Oct. 1840, SL. An excellent discussion of early foreigners, including Davis, is in Bancroft, *History*, III, 107-21.

CHAPTER II

APPRENTICESHIP

A TOTALLY DIFFERENT description of William's adopted country from the attractive scene he portrayed for his distant friends may be gained from the writings of Commodore Charles Wilkes, commander of the first American naval expedition to the California coast in 1841. After describing the site of the future San Francisco as scarcely "calculated to produce a favourable impression upon a stranger," he remarked that the small settlement consisted merely of a few wind-lashed frame structures: Spear's store, a billiard room and bar, a beached poop cabin of a ship, a blacksmith's shop, and "some out buildings." Wilkes summed up his condemning description with the remark that Yerba Buena was "anything but beautiful." He found the locality equally drab in a political sense. Though prepared for "anarchy and confusion," he was surprised by "a total absence of all government." Certainly Davis, who was young, relatively insensitive to inconveniences, and enjoying himself, had a more optimistic view of sand-blown San Francisco.

Other descriptions of the peninsula in that early day, however, resemble Wilkes's dire account. One traveler at the time of his visit could count only four permanent residents at Yerba Buena, including Davis and his uncle.[1] Actually the locale had not changed appreciably since 1829 when the trader Alfred Robinson found the presidio of the future city of San Francisco "in a most ruinous state." In his book, *Life In California*, Robinson

[1]Charles Wilkes, *Narrative of the United States Exploring Expedition during the years 1838, 1839, 1840, 1841, 1842* (Philadelphia, 1844), V, 152, 158-59; William Dane Phelps, *Fore and Aft; or, Leaves from the life of an old sailor* (Boston, 1871), p. 252.

21

further described Mission Dolores as propped up by some decaying walls and topped by a crumbling tile roof that "well accorded with the bleak and cheerless scenery with which it is surrounded."

Though such early commentators spoke in unflattering terms of the tiny settlement by the Pacific, few of them doubted its economic future. Even the pessimistic Wilkes became enthusiastic over what he called the greatest natural harbor in the world. He wrote with appreciation of the vast hinterland beyond the estuary where Davis and his uncle lived and worked. The commodore also looked favorably upon the operation of Spear's mill, noting that he manufactured soap and supplied the expedition with inexpensive pork.[2]

Davis, too, had been learning of California's superiority in agricultural wealth over his native Hawaii. He continued to be impressed by the league-wide private grants that bore such names as Santa Rosa, La Boca de la Cañada del Pinole, San Pablo, San Antonio, San Leandro, and San Lorenzo Bajo, ranchos which were stocked with herds of cattle and horses that stretched as far across the landscape as the eye could reach.[3] As he visited first one and then another of the owners of these estates whose land included both the cedar- and pine-covered valleys inland and the rolling hills along the coast, his affection grew for the country and for the people around him. He learned, above all, how to deal with such grandees as Mariano Guadalupe Vallejo, the dominant landholder and political figure in northern California.

Davis extended his uncle's contacts far inland, regularly traveling northward to New Helvetia to trade with Sutter. Still further north, Davis traded for furs with the trapper and hunter John Sinclair who, at his suggestion, had established himself on the right bank of the American River. Attempting to gain a measure of revenge upon the man who had advised him to make

[2]Spear also supplied Wilkes's group with staples when it went to Sutter's fort, incidentally complaining vigorously about the low prices paid by the U. S. Government. See Spear to Larkin, Nov. 3, Dec. 7, 1841, LP.

[3]No studies of the quality of Robert Glass Cleland, *Cattle On A Thousand Hills, Southern California, 1850-1880* (San Marino, 1941, 1951) or William W. Robinson, *Ranchos Become Cities* (Pasadena, 1939), have yet appeared concerning California's northern ranchos.

a home in such a wilderness, Sinclair once invited Davis to become his guest and then sought to sell him a number of ferocious grizzly bears which he had trapped. He also expressed the hope that Davis might one day "know the pleasure of letter writing in the midst of myriads of mosquitoes while with every line you wrote you would be obliged to lay down your pen to enjoy the luxury of scratching." In establishing relations with landholders around the bay such as he developed with the lonely hunter at the forks of the Sacramento, the trader came to be trusted even by those who held unpaid claims against his uncle.[4]

But Davis's contacts were not only with permanent residents. Presently his path crossed that of an international traveler. Eugène Duflot de Mofras, on a trip of observation for the French government, stayed at Spear's establishment, where visitors to Yerba Buena frequently lodged. Although Davis did not realize it Duflot de Mofras was engaged in something more than a pleasure tour. One historian considers Davis naïve for not perceiving imperialistic overtones in the Frenchman's travels. But Davis, who had little background in political subtlety, did not detect the foreign visitor's designs upon California. A boy in his teens could easily be misled by the finesse of a cultured, multi-lingual Frenchman. The suave Duflot de Mofras was a striking contrast to the brusque Sutter, the only other foreigner whom Davis knew.[5]

Nathan Spear, who feared the motives of Duflot de Mofras and the occasional Englishmen who visited San Francisco Bay, was not so unsuspecting as his nephew and reported the movements of such strangers to Wilkes. Impressed by the trader's powers of observation, the latter promised to nominate him to be the future United States Consul at Yerba Buena, a promise that never bore fruit.

Like Commodore Wilkes before him, Duflot de Mofras, during his visit of several months, accompanied Davis on a number of

[4]Sinclair to Davis, Aug. 17, 1840, SL, and May 27, 1840, UCLA; Phelps, *Fore and Aft*, p. 247; Juan Perry to M. G. Vallejo, Aug. 23, 1839, Vallejo Documents, VIII, Bancroft Library. Hereafter cited as BL.

[5]See Rufus Kay Wyllys, "French Imperialists in California," *Calif. Hist. Soc. Quarterly*, VIII (1929), 124-25.

trips around San Francisco Bay. On one of these excursions the launch *Isabel* grounded the two on a mud flat. Though the youth explained that the incoming tide would soon float them off, the excitable Frenchman became impatient, plunged overboard, and swam ashore fully clothed. Dripping wet, he appeared at Spear's house on foot some hours after Davis had arrived and had to face the youth's good-humored raillery.

In their printed memoirs both Wilkes and Duflot de Mofras recalled many pleasant moments which they had spent at Yerba Buena with Davis and his neighbors. For their part these resident Americans, huddled together during the 1840's in that remote "village of mint," found the company of such visitors extremely entertaining, especially on fog-shrouded and lonely winter nights. To young Davis, perhaps more than to any of his companions, their stories of the outside world served to break the monotony of those long evenings.[6]

As time passed, he absorbed many of the California trader's most necessary lessons: how to evade the unreasonable duties which the government of California imposed on incoming goods, how to buy and sell, and how to deal with competitors both friendly and unfriendly. Because tariff charges frequently ran as high as eighty or one hundred per cent of the value of a ship's cargo, local traders found it greatly to their advantage to become smugglers. In their evasion of duties, Davis and Spear, like other resident foreigners, were following in the footsteps of an earlier generation of Boston mariners to which Davis's own father had belonged. Whether morally justifiable or not, the practice of avoiding at least some of the confiscatory charges enabled these traders to deliver badly needed Boston goods to California's rancheros at prices which they could afford to pay.[7]

William Heath Davis, like other Americans then in California,

[6]Duflot de Mofras, *Exploration du territoire de L'Orégon des Californies et de la mer Vermeille, exécutée pendant les années 1840, 1841 et 1842* (Paris, 1844).

[7]Underhill, *Cowhides*, p. 21; *75 Years*, pp. 156, 176; Davis's comments about smuggling are in various MSS of the Davis Collection, Henry E. Huntington Library, San Marino, Calif.; see also Bancroft, *History*, IV, 82; Adele Ogden, "New England Traders in Spanish and Mexican California," *Greater America, Essays in Honor of Herbert Eugene Bolton* (Berkeley, 1945), pp. 395-415.

helped to alter the traditional trading methods that Spain had established on the California coast. Since the late eighteenth century Spain's frontier outposts had often been provisioned by trading companies licensed through the crown. In keeping with this tradition, even after Mexico achieved independence from Spain, a trading agreement was earlier signed by the California authorities with the English firm of McCulloch, Hartnell & Company. Consummated in the 1820's, before Spear's and Davis's time, this contract had not only begun the prosperous hide and tallow trade, but it had also helped legalize future Yankee trading in California.

Under this agreement the missions had furnished the bulk of the hides, tallow, and steer horns desired by the English company. In return for receiving such local products, the firm was allowed to trade one cargo of finished goods in California each year. By the thirties, following their secularization by the Mexican government, the missions had been eliminated as important participants in trade. Ambitious Yankee middlemen—principally resident merchants like Spear and Davis—rapidly filled that void. They replaced the supercargoes of McCulloch, Hartnell & Company who had once distributed goods on land from their ships. The new American trading arrangement especially pleased the rancheros, for they were no longer dependent upon the uncertain arrival of trading vessels. Ship captains also found the new system to their advantage. They could now load and unload their vessels at central collecting points, rather than at numerous and sometimes dangerous landfalls scattered along the coast. The Yankee storekeeper had, thus, come to play a significant role in the life of each pueblo.[8]

In the Boston-Honolulu-California portion of their trading activities, however, Davis and his uncle encountered stiff competition. From the 1820's until virtually the outbreak of the Mexican War one large Boston firm, Bryant, Sturgis & Company, maintained a chain of ships plying the sea lanes between that harbor, California, and even China. This firm alone carried

[8]See Adele Ogden, "Hides and Tallow: McCulloch, Hartnell and Company, 1822-1828," *Calif. Hist. Soc. Quarterly*, VI (1927), 254-64; Susanna Bryant Dakin, *The Lives of William Hartnell* (Stanford, Calif., 1949), pp. 49, 64-69, 122.

probably half a million hides (for shoes) from California to New England, untold quantities of tallow (for candles) to Lima, and tons of cow horns (for shoe buttons) to the east coast of the United States. Naturally Davis came to know that important company's many representatives intimately.[9] Other sizable firms from Boston he learned to respect included Marshall & Wildes and William Appleton & Company, both of which kept several vessels on the California coast. These large New England firms and traders, with whom Davis and Spear found themselves in competition, helped establish the first substantial liaison between California, New England, and Hawaii.

Still another source of competition which Spear and Davis met—and for a time the fiercest of all—was furnished by the Hudson's Bay Company. That firm established a post in San Francisco in 1841 following a personal inspection of the site by its chief, Dr. John McLoughlin. Called the "White Headed Eagle" throughout the West, he entrusted management of the company's post at Yerba Buena to his son-in-law, William G. Rae, a good friend of Davis's. Rae's headquarters were located in the same block as the town bar and the convenience of the tap room encouraged Rae in his fondness for liquor. According to Davis, Rae was also unfaithful to his wife while at Yerba Buena; he ended his career by committing suicide. After his death the Hudson's Bay Company ceased its operations in California. While this freed Davis and Spear of a major competitor, they regretted the loss of the one good card player that Yerba Buena boasted.[10]

[9]See letter and account books of Bryant, Sturgis & Co., Baker Library MS. 766, Harvard University. Excellent studies of the California trade are Cleland's *Cattle*, Adele Ogden, *The California Sea Otter Trade, 1784-1848* (Berkeley, 1941) and her articles: "Alfred Robinson, New England Merchant in Mexican California," *Calif. Hist. Soc. Quarterly*, XXIII (1944), 193-218, and "Boston Hide Droghers Along California Shores," *Calif. Hist. Soc. Quarterly*, VIII (1929), 289-305.

[10]On the Hudson's Bay Company's California operations see Huntington MS. DA1 (227) and Robert Glass Cleland, *This Reckless Breed of Men: The Trappers and Fur Traders of the Southwest* (New York, 1950), pp. 311-43; Alice Bay Maloney, "Peter Skene Ogden's Trapping Expedition to the Gulf of California, 1829-30," *Calif. Hist. Soc. Quarterly*, XIX (1940), 308-16; John S. Galbraith, "A Note on the British Fur Trade in California, 1821-1846," *Pacific Historical Review*, XXIV (1955), 253-60.

With the Hudson's Bay Company no longer an active bidder for furs in the interior, Spear instructed Davis to buy more of the pelts formerly sold it by trappers like John Sinclair. To purchase such furs Davis did not usually need to carry money with him. The same condition prevailed in trading with rancheros. In accordance with an almost invariable practice, they were accustomed to barter their hides and tallow for the manufactured goods supplied by Davis.

In such exchanges prices varied widely depending, in part, upon duties which importers had to pay. When, for example, customs fees reached $18,000 on one cargo, Davis and his uncle were forced to charge $15 for a pair of boots, $3 for silk stockings, and $4 a pound for linen thread. Even when prices ran high the Californians were more than pleased to receive Spear's valuable Hawaiian imports of cocoanuts, coffee, sugar, sperm-whale oil, and sweet potatoes. In return, they traded him wheat at $3 a fanega (1½ bushels), cattle at $5 a head, and steer hides at approximately $1 each.

Quantities of these hides, "California banknotes," were usually brought from the province's interior in a "green" state or, at best, carelessly dried. After overflowing Spear's store, these smelly skins sometimes spilled even into Davis's bedroom. Part of his job was to help soak them in sea water, then to stretch them on the ground, and to peg them fast with wooden stakes. When the hides were dry, he sprinkled them with salt and folded them lengthwise with the hair out. Finally the skins were packed into the holds of waiting ships some of which held as many as 30,000 hides. With them went accumulations of tallow that had been melted and poured into large bags made of cowhide. In all these operations—buying and selling, curing hides, and arranging for the transfer of hides and tallow to waiting ships—Davis played an active role.

While in the employ of his uncle Davis learned also to respect the competition posed by the whalers who visited California ports. They often remained away from their home ports as long as four years and were accustomed to trade excess supplies with California rancheros, particularly on the eve of re-outfitting their vessels for the homeward voyage to New England. Because they

27

undercut prices which regular traders asked for their goods, Davis adopted his uncle's unfriendly attitude toward these storm-tossed seamen.[11]

Spear's store did, however, become a popular gathering place for many other kinds of people. His customers included *Californios* carrying chickens under their arms or herding pigs into Spear's corral back of the store, overland fur traders, and beach-combing sailors who had escaped the harsh discipline of New England masters. Rancheros also came to buy silks and calicoes for their wives and boots and tobacco for themselves. At Spear's store his nephew learned not to extend credit to transient "floaters" who often spent their money for liquor and the company of Indian squaws or half-breed women.

Spear had amiable relations with most traders and rancheros but he could not get along with Sutter. The Baron of the Sacramento not only defaulted on his debts, but often brought into Yerba Buena his unmanageable retinue of Indians and Hawaiian Kanakas whose presence angered Spear beyond endurance. Once accused of detaining one of Sutter's servants, Kanaka James, Spear sent the boy back to his master with the following sarcastic note:

I must say Captain Sutter that I am indeed surprised that you should for a moment entertain a thought that I should keep your Kanaka at my house for any other purpose than that of returning him to you whenever proper opportunity offered.

Spear ultimately terminated his correspondence with Sutter on this score by the sentence: "You will excuse me when I say that further commerce must end with you." But in spite of Spear's exasperation, the merchant could not bring his commercial dealings with New Helvetia to such an abrupt end and clerk Davis had to continue to write long letters urging the Swiss to pay his debts.

Sutter did partially repay Spear by catching, smoking, and

[11]In contrast to the attitude of Spear and Davis, Larkin at Monterey ran advertisements in eastern newspapers designed to lure whalers to that snug harbor. These men of Nantucket and New Bedford, in fact, left behind at Monterey a whalebone sidewalk as a token of their appreciation for its shelter. Underhill, *Cowhides*, p. 67; Spear to Larkin, Nov. 3, Dec. 7, 1841, LP.

shipping downriver large numbers of salmon.[12] He furnished Spear and Davis with Indian helpers and supplied lumber for their cooper to make into barrel staves. Sutter also sent beaver pelts downstream, especially when he wanted to buy saddles for his own use and beads and jewelry to trade with the Indians. He knew that Spear and Davis were usually anxious to obtain the red clay of New Helvetia for use as a base for paint and he frequently included quantities of it in his shipments. When, however, Sutter sent them bags of impure, colored earth, at an exorbitant price, they lost all patience with him.[13]

Despite the temporary loss of one of their best customers Spear and Davis prospered. Into their warehouses flowed in an ever increasing stream the wealth of pastoral California, the wares of the Orient, and the goods of New England. Benefiting from the breakdown of the mission system, these "warm-water Yankees" reaped rich rewards from their all-year stock of goods. Almost everyone profited from their activities except Mexico's customs collectors and their importance to California's economy could not be denied even by such officials. One historian has asserted that these pre-pioneers who settled California long before the first overland wagon parties crossed the plains "deserve an attention that has seldom been accorded them."[14]

Davis would certainly remember one of these men. He was extremely fortunate to be trained by his uncle who not only knew the art of trading but who also understood the economic aspects of the culture in which he lived. As Nathan Spear's apprentice, William became familiar with the economy of the territory and this, combined with his appreciation of the people, was to stand him in good stead for a number of years. In his own person he came to represent a blending of California's Spanish and Anglo-Saxon culture.

[12]Spear to Sutter, Apr. 16, 22, 1840, SLB; Spear to Ygnacio Martinez, July 22, 1841 and to Sutter, July 22, 1840 and Jan. 1, 1841, SLB. In 75 Years, p. 162, Davis credits Spear with beginning the first salmon fishery on the Pacific Coast.

[13]Spear to Sutter, June 18, July 22, Oct. 12, 1840, Jan. 1, 18, Mar. 16, May 14, 1841, SLB; Sutter to Davis, Apr. 22, 1844, BL; New Helvetia Diary, ed. William F. Swasey (San Francisco, 1939), pp. ix, 1, 60, mention Davis's and Spear's relations with Sutter.

[14]John Walton Caughey, California (New York, 1940), p. 240.

CHAPTER III

TRADER AND SUPERCARGO

BECAUSE OF HIS deep affection for
California Davis wished to be considered an *hijo del pais*—a true
son of the country. In 1840 to strengthen his position he expe-
diently sought Mexican citizenship. To his surprise he learned
that his arrest during the "Graham Affair" barred him from
becoming a Mexican national. The governor of California did,
however, finally concede Davis a permanent passport. After
paying a fee of one dollar for this handsome beribboned document Davis, already known as "Don Guillermo," could legally
travel throughout the province as though he were a citizen.[1]

His Hawaiian friends refused to believe that he would remain
at Yerba Buena. Imploring him to come to his senses they tanta-
lized him with descriptions of the *poi*, the moonlight, and the
young women in the islands. But Davis wanted, more than anything else, to start a business of his own in California. In fact
his success in working with his uncle's clientele was speeding
the day when he would leave Spear's employ.

In January 1842, Spear agreed to allow his nephew to join
a friend's shipping firm where an opportunity existed for the
young man to move eventually into a business of his own.
Davis's new employer was a widely known shipper, the friendly
Captain John Paty. As owner of the bark *Don Quixote* he had
long had his eye on Spear's nephew, whom he desired as his
supercargo. Though still only twenty Davis, after accepting the
captain's offer, became the supervisor of the mercantile operations of a vessel that sailed regularly from the Hawaiian Islands

[1]Calif. Dept. of State Papers, XVII, 62, XX, 9, BL. Passport of Guillermo H.
Davis, Mar. 17, 1841, is in the possession of H. F. Bruning, Palo Alto, Calif.;
letter transmitting it is by Eugenio Montenegro to Davis, Mar. 18, 1841, UCLA.

to the mainland of North America. Three to four months were required to peddle such a ship's cargo of goods along the coastline from Yerba Buena to San Diego. Upon joining the ship Davis accepted responsibility for its sales and purchases in California.

He was expected to resort to any means to evade Mexican customs duties. Supercargoes in California waters often bribed officials to approve short invoices, cached goods away into false linings built within a ship's hull, and secreted merchandise among non-dutiable ship's stores. Frequently they transferred goods from vessels that had not paid duty to others already cleared through customs. Traders who engaged in such swindling spoke of leaving their consciences at Cape Horn.

Davis's superior, Captain Paty, also evaded customs duties by secreting cargoes at remote landfalls or by engaging in offshore smuggling. On one occasion Davis politely helped detain a customs guard detailed aboard the *Don Quixote* at Yerba Buena to prevent such smuggling. While the guard relaxed in a cabin stocked with cigars and liquor, Davis stored some $20,000 worth of dutiable goods in Spear's warehouse. Then, after dropping the sentry ashore, the ship went to Monterey for its official inspection and clearance. When the *Don Quixote* returned to Yerba Buena, Davis retrieved the original cargo from its hiding place.

By 1843 Paty's operations had become so entwined with those of various other traders that he formed the firm of Paty, McKinley & Fitch. Henry Delano Fitch combined talents as a ranchero near San Diego with his position as the firm's resident agent at that port. The third partner, James McKinley, was a young Scot and, like Davis, had been a traveling trader. Davis became one of the firm's silent members. He was now associated with an alert group of men who would prove invaluable to one who wanted to gain experience and money for a business of his own.[2]

Traveling for Paty along the California coast brought Davis

[2]Mrs. F. H. Day, "Sketches of The Early Settlers of California. Capt. John Paty," *The Hesperian*, III (1859), 289-300.

into a wider circle of even more important people than he had known while working for his uncle. For example, when California's capital was prematurely taken in 1842 by Commodore Thomas Ap Catesby Jones's American Pacific squadron, Davis was able to meet the controversial naval figure. He and Paty arrived at Monterey aboard the *Don Quixote* only a few days after Jones, on the mistaken assumption that the United States was at war with Mexico, had hauled down the Mexican flag flying over the town's customs house. To smooth over the affair, Larkin, the American consular representative at Monterey gave the embarrassed Jones and his officers a military ball to which the leading lights of the locality were invited. Paty and his young supercargo were among the guests and at the ball William met María Jesús Estudillo. Although Davis at this time had only a passing acquaintance with the Estudillos, he knew their prestige among California's families and was delighted to have met the gracious young woman who was the center of much attention. He was also flattered to have been invited to a celebration of such importance; the invitation was indicative not only of his increased prestige but of the impression of maturity that he imparted to others.[3]

In recognition of his new stature Davis was intrusted with more responsibility at his home base at Yerba Buena. While the *Don Quixote* formed the mainstay of Paty, McKinley & Fitch, the firm also maintained at Yerba Buena a tile-roofed adobe headquarters named "Casa Grande." Like Abel Stearns's "Casa de San Pedro" in southern California, this anchor on land was a collection point for hides and tallow. From their Yerba Buena base, where they gathered and prepared hides for shipment to New England, the partners alternated as agents on shore. When it was his turn to collect hides Davis erected a large wooden hide shed on the beach in front of the adobe. Thereafter visiting vessels,

[3]Davis believed Commodore Jones to be a genial man who had made an honest mistake because of incorrect information. His capture of California's capital involved the temporary incarceration of the Estudillo girl. She had been sailing northward aboard the Mexican *Joven Guipuzcoana* when elements of Jones's squadron overtook that vessel and ordered its master to heave to and surrender its passengers. When Jones met María's father at Monterey he tried to make amends. See *75 Years*, pp. 113-19 and "Glimpses," p. 98.

shallow enough in draft to get close to the shore, could load and unload at high tide onto a short pier at Davis's front door.

Without then knowing it Davis and his associates were among the last of a generation of California hide and tallow merchants; but they were among the most successful. Davis helped develop so large a coastwise traffic in hides that in mid-1844 his firm had collected some 4,000 for shipment to New England. Davis and his friends were selling so many skins to the eastern trading firms that their business bulked even larger than Nathan Spear's.[4]

Davis had accumulated a good deal of money and looked forward to the day when he could prove his success to his family. He got that chance when Captain Paty took him on a business trip to Hawaii. He bought for his island relatives the costly presents he had dreamed of bestowing upon them; fine silks and even horses replaced the simple sea shells he had once picked up on California's beaches to send his mother.[5]

On this and subsequent trips to the Hawaiian Islands with Captain Paty he helped select merchandise for later sale in California, for reshipment to Mexico, to the Columbia River territory, or even to remote English and Russian possessions further north. In choosing such supplies Davis earned a reputation for shrewdness; for this reason, and because he was companionable, Paty was anxious to have him along on trips to Hawaii.[6]

Whenever Davis was not in the islands, letters kept him informed of the latest Hawaiian news. His brother, Robert, frequently sent trade information which he passed on to American Consul Larkin at Monterey. In this way Larkin learned of such events as overstocking of the Honolulu market, recurring rumors about war with Mexico or Britain, and complaints over Hawaiian import restrictions.[7]

Robert usually had advice to offer William as well as trading tips. Reminding him once that his island friends believed "there

[4]See William Appleton & Company to George Mellus, Feb. 26, 1851, Gordon-Dexter Collection, XXXVII, Baker Library, Harvard University.

[5]I. H. Everett to Davis, Sept. 27, 1843, SL.

[6]Reynolds to Spear, May 23, 1842, UCLA; *Temperance Advocate, and Seamen's Friend* (Honolulu), May 20, 1843.

[7]R. G. Davis to Larkin, May 27, 1842, LP.

was not a person on the coast so well suited for trading," he urged William to enter business on his own. Plans for a California partnership with his brother were on Robert's mind when he further advised William to buy a Yerba Buena commercial site, a boat, and even a California ranch. William was not receptive to Robert's persistent suggestions about starting a business. He did, however, follow his brother's advice to the extent of purchasing a San Francisco waterfront site which became the foundation of his extensive real estate holdings. This early purchase proved crucially important to his later fortune and was to distinguish him from dozens of other traders who simply drifted through the future San Francisco.[8]

In his contacts with the islands, William found himself obliged to act as domestic arbiter *in absentia*. The intimacy which once existed between the two brothers faded somewhat as William's success grew. Robert's letters, occasionally tinctured with envy, showed that he lacked William's tact in handling their indomitable mother. Each time a flare-up occurred between the temperamental Hannah and the Hawaiian government, she turned to her younger son for help. When, for example, the British temporarily took over the Hawaiian Islands in 1843, it was William who protested for her against confiscation of family properties. On this occasion he was especially bitter because the missionary-influenced Hawaiian government, whose members had long disliked the Davises, did very little to prevent their loss of real estate.[9]

As if to complicate William's relations with his family, his mother was improvident on many occasions. In 1844, much to the disgust of both brothers, she slaughtered about a hundred of the family's cattle herd. Her childish squandering of the proceeds on unneeded jewelry injected discord into the Davises' already disturbed affairs.[10]

[8]R. G. Davis to Davis, July 8, 20, Aug. 2, Oct. 31, Dec. 6, 14, 1842, Jan. 14, 1843, and Jones to Davis, Aug. 20, 1843, SL.

[9]Office of the British Commission for the Government of the Sandwich Islands to Davis, Apr. 21, 1843, SL; R. G. Davis to Davis, Nov. 4, Dec. 22, 1843, Jan. 10, 31, 1844, SL.

[10]R. G. Davis to Davis, Nov. 4, Dec. 22, 1843, Feb. 26, May 28, 1844, Apr. 28, June 29, 1846, and John G. Lewis to Davis, June 28, 1846, SL.

34

In his writings the novelist Jack London inferred that women like Hannah may have constituted a social type in Hawaii. In his book *On the Makaloa Mat* he stated, "Unlike the women of most warm races, those of Hawaii age well and nobly." Such an appraisal would definitely have applied to Hannah who, after being forsaken by Davis's stepfather, kept herself youthful despite a turbulent personal life. She and her daughter, Elizabeth, caused continual gossip among the missionaries because of their taste for expensive clothes, offensive dancing, and their habit of "forming intimacies with strangers," which especially disturbed William. A vestige of his New England heritage made it difficult for him unreservedly to accept his mother's Hawaiian viewpoints.[11]

Despite continued family disturbances in Hawaii William tried to keep his mind on the California commerce in which he was engaged. Luckily Captain Paty allowed him to carry on an increasing amount of trading on his own. Because he enjoyed good relations with the Yerba Buena customs collector—who lived rent free in the firm's adobe store—that official permitted the young trader the unusual convenience of employing the customs boat at night to transact business with visiting ships. This concession obviously carried with it still another privilege, safety from the law. Thereby assured of uninterrupted operations Davis, under cover of darkness, often landed high-dutied calicoes and cottons stuffed in wooden watercasks. As he later described this trafficking, each end of the cask was "filled with Boston pilot bread to the depth of eighteen or twenty inches." Bread, a duty-free commodity, could be landed legally because a scarcity of ovens ashore had made the staff of life all too rare. Other traders, of course, also resorted to this ruse in order to land goods, but none with the immunity that Davis had arranged for himself. Such covert trading was so profitable that it netted him $2,000 to $3,000 in two years, in addition to his regular salary and commission from Paty.

Among the foreigners with whom he and the captain were trading were Davis's cousin, William Goodwin Dana of Nipomo, and further south, at San Diego, Henry Delano Fitch, a partner

[11]Reynolds to Davis, May 14, 1844, June 28, Sept. 22, 1846, and R. G. Davis to Davis, Nov. 4, 1843, Apr. 28, Sept. 24, 1846, SL; Davis to Reynolds, Aug. 20, 1846, SL.

in Paty's firm. Davis and Paty represented Fitch in the north and he handled business for them near San Diego. Fitch usually sent saddles, silk garters, shirts, spurs, tobacco, and unbleached muslin called *manta*, and brandy (known locally as *aguardiente de uva*) which Davis traded for northern beaver skins, or hides and tallow. Fitch, in turn, used these items to barter with the rancheros or to buy supplies from visiting ships.

Davis still looked forward to an independent career and continued to meet people in a position to render him aid. He was, for instance, fortunate to meet José de la Guerra y Noriega of Santa Barbara, perhaps the wealthiest man in the province. When the dignified Spaniard learned that William was the son of Captain Davis, with whom the old man had traded many years before, Davis Jr. was immediately able to sell de la Guerra some $10,000 worth of goods, the largest quantity of eastern merchandise he had yet sold. Once he got back to Yerba Buena he boasted to all his acquaintances that he was one of the few Americans ever allowed to see de la Guerra's treasure of baskets filled to their brims with gold doubloons. Davis did not realize that Yankees like himself were already participating in a process by which the Californians were transferring such wealth to a growing minority of foreign invaders.

In view of his increasing solvency many wondered why the young man did not marry. But Davis appeared shy in matters of the heart. On one occasion Fitch michieviously hinted that he should admit that he was pursuing a woman of dubious repute named Juanita. To this the ordinarily equable Davis replied by the next post: "I cannot imagine who should have reported such a false report and to an infernal whore . . . I want to get something to maintain a wife with first." Davis was convinced that because his trips for Paty kept him continually on the move, he should not marry until he was more permanently settled.[12]

His travels took him far into California's interior and as he paced off the miles on horseback between missions and ranchos

[12]Fitch to Davis, Jan. 31, Apr. 27, 1844, Davis to Fitch, June 10, 1844, SL; Fitch to Davis, Mar. 18, Apr. 4, 1844, Mar. 7, 1845, UCLA. For a picture of Davis at sea see Chester S. Lyman, *Around the Horn to the Sandwich Islands and California, 1845-1850* . . . ed. Frederick J. Teggart (New Haven, 1924), p. 202.

he had ample time to think about his future. More important to him than the numerous young women he had met in recent years was the business experience he was gaining. The many inland trips he made for Paty in order to sell the *Don Quixote's* goods acquainted him with problems involved in conducting a mercantile business and furnished him opportunities for recreation with new-found friends.[13]

There was, for example, Hugo Reid whom Davis first encountered in the early 1840's while traveling in southern California. He visited the engaging Scot at Rancho Santa Anita where Reid lived with an Indian wife on her dower of land. Intending to sell them cloth off the *Don Quixote*, anchored at nearby San Pedro, he was surprised to learn that Reid, a castaway on the edge of a wilderness, was a trained accountant. Davis subsequently employed his new friend to audit his company's ledgers. With the account books which Davis thereafter lugged to Santa Anita, he usually carried *panocha*, hard sugar, which Reid's wife craved. There was no rancho in California that Davis relished visiting more than Reid's remote, oak-covered site. Davis made the trip to Santa Anita many times, sometimes staying a week or more. His description of the visits ultimately helped to dispel the gossip that white men like Reid pursued slovenly lives as "squaw" men in California's interior.[14]

Trading trips southward frequently took Davis to San Diego where he usually remained for as much as a month to visit with Fitch and the many rancheros there who requested supplies. As a matter of routine he canvassed such establishments as the Rancho San Jacinto Nuevo belonging to the Aguirre family, the Argüellos' Tia Juana hacienda, and the Pedrorenas' Rancho El Cajon. When in southern California Davis never failed to take goods for sale also to Juan Bandini's Rancho Jurupa, and to the ranchos of the Yorbas, Sepulvedas, and Lugos near Los

[13]Comandancia General de California, July 3, 1844, Vallejo Documents, XII, 45, BL.

[14]Susanna Bryant Dakin, *A Scotch Paisano; Hugo Reid's life in California, 1832-1852, derived from his correspondence* (Berkeley, 1939), pp. 70-73 utilized Davis's excellent description. See also H. P. Reid to Davis, Jan. 26, 1845, SL, and Fitch to Davis, Feb. 18, 1845, UCLA.

Angeles. While traveling through this southern vineyard country the trader sought out for his Hawaiian customers the best *aguardiente* and fortified wine to be found.

As Davis journeyed north after long trips to southern California he stopped to trade at each of the missions as well as at ranchos enroute. As Santa Barbara he was always sure of good sales to his friend de la Guerra; further north at Monterey it was the Munras, Soberanes, and Estrada families and the Bernals of San Jose who usually absorbed the last of his dwindling supplies of Boston and Honolulu imports. When the *Don Quixote*—which followed its supercargo offshore with the cargoes that he required—ran out of goods, the ship returned to its home base at Yerba Buena.

On his many trips the families with whom he stayed entertained the friendly young bachelor with amusements characteristic of the pastoral society of the 1840's. He loved to join rancheros in strawberry hunts far into the countryside. Bull and bear fights were still popular California sports and he attended these events whenever possible. Before taking leave of a family Davis was often given a *merienda* with *carne asada*, meat roasted on spits over a bed of coals. Usually accompanying the barbecue were such activities as turkey shooting, horse racing, or cockfighting, all of which Davis thoroughly enjoyed.

But the California of his youth was not always the scene of such frivolity. The ambitions of its *politicos,* added to the sectionalism of the north versus the south of the province, frequently produced social disorder that was at least disturbing if seldom dangerous. In 1845 Davis and his associates became involved in the last of a series of minor political revolts. This was a clash between the headstrong former governor, Juan B. Alvarado, and his newly appointed successor, Manuel Micheltorena. Davis was trading in Los Angeles when the revolt against Micheltorena occurred. He was requested by an American friend there, Alexander Bell, who felt compelled to join Alvarado's "army" which was massing near Los Angeles, to take charge of his store and, indeed, to look after his wife. Like Abel Stearns, who saw no sense in these activities, Davis tried to quiet the aroused foreign population of Los Angeles. Among the most frightened Ameri-

cans was Bell's wife, who feared she might become a widow over-
night. Because Bell had left a sizable sum of money in his store
safe, Davis was uneasy; he had been entrusted not only with
another man's wife but also with his earthly savings. Unlike
Bell, who participated in the later American conquest of California, Davis showed little interest in either military or political
battles. Throughout his lifetime he left to others the combatant's
role.[15]

After this last of California's seriocomic political fracases ended
(the only dead on either side was one mule), Davis's fellow
trader, McKinley, mediated the dispute. Despite its bloodlessness
and brevity, ending with the defeat of Micheltorena, both fac-
tions in the disturbance had enlisted many of California's most
prominent persons. Bell and other Americans were annoyed because both Sutter and General Vallejo had joined Micheltorena's
forces. But Davis, like Sutter, feared Alvarado even more than
Micheltorena and the half-breed irregulars, *cholos*, who had
come north from Mexico with the unpopular official. Davis
remembered how Alvarado had, but a few years before, impris-
oned many Americans including his uncle and himself. Perhaps
Davis's and Paty's partiality for the unhorsed governor, Micheltorena, was responsible for their being commissioned to transport
him and his troops back to Mexico on the *Don Quixote*.[16]

With the "battle" over, Davis and Abel Stearns joined the
participants from each camp such as John Marsh, John Bidwell,
Charles Flügge, and Bell at Los Angeles. Yet, their sipping of Don
Luís Vignes' wines late into the night did not lessen the animosity
which some still held for Sutter. Of this event Davis's stepfather
confidentially wrote Larkin: "Sutter has fallen, and I think, like
Lucifer, never will rise again." Davis must have thought to himself
how in this instance, as in various others, Sutter's durability was

[15]*75 Years*, pp. 28-29; Benjamin S. Harrison, *Fortune Favors The Brave; the
life and times of Horace Bell, pioneer Californian* (Los Angeles, 1953), p. 29.

[16]While evacuating Micheltorena southward, Paty and Davis received with
mixed feelings Micheltorena's expression of regret that he had not favored them
with land grants during his term of office as he had John Sutter, John Bidwell,
Job Dye, Dr. John Marsh, and Theodor Cordua. See John Paty to Larkin, Feb.
25, 1845, LP; Davis to Larkin, Apr. 1, 1845, LP; Calif. Dept. of State Papers, VI,
151, BL; *75 Years*, pp. 132-34.

39

underrated by many. He and Spear had learned by experience that Sutter could "roll with the punches."

Following the ouster of Micheltorena, Davis learned of a recent decision made by his uncle that would deprive him of the almost daily counsel and advice which had partly accounted for his own success. Nathan Spear, who had recently been ill, announced the abandonment of his Yerba Buena business. Much to Davis's regret, he still did not have enough money to take over Spear's store. And his uncle could lend him none, for he needed it in order to join an eccentric Englishman and friend of long standing, Dr. Edward Turner Bale, on a ranching venture in the Napa Valley. Although the doctor was a "boozer" and something of a scamp, William's uncle and aunt were attracted by his offer of partnership. Spear and Bale were a real contrast to one another, but, much to William's pleasure, they agreed perfectly in business matters. In addition both men shared a smattering of pharmaceutical knowledge which was valuable in the interior valleys. Spear had not only dispensed medicine in his Yerba Buena store, but had also on occasion served as doctor to the sick. At Napa, in addition to continuing the sale of drugs, Spear became a judge and interested himself in quicksilver mining and the development, with Bale, of a saw and flour mill, still standing near Saint Helena. Whenever Bale sent flour from their mill to Yerba Buena for him to sell, he usually requested payment in brandy so, as he once put it, "I can have the pleasure of drinking your good health."[17]

Davis continued to work for Captain Paty, and after his uncle had departed Yerba Buena, he supplanted Spear as its best-known trader. Because of the wealth of experience which he had learned from both these men he was soon asked to form the business firm that most young men could only dream of commencing. While in Honolulu late in 1845 a partnership was proposed by Captain Paty himself. Paty, who had just bought out his associates, admired Davis's talents so much that he offered him the chance to buy a share of his business. On the verge of accepting this offer, he received still another bid from the English commercial house

[17]E. T. Bale to Davis, Nov. 12, 1846, SL; Bancroft, *History*, II, 730; Dean Albertson, "Dr. Edward Turner Bale, Incorrigible Californio," *Calif. Hist. Soc. Quarterly*, XXVIII (1949), 259-69.

of Starkey, Janion & Company—a proposition which included furnishing him a vessel for trade along the California coast. He declined both offers, however, in favor of a third proposal made by two Hawaiian merchants, Eliab and Hiram Grimes, whom he knew well and in whom he then had much faith. By joining them in a partnership he thereby began a sometimes annoying but an exceedingly profitable relationship that lasted almost until the California Gold Rush.[18]

William Heath Davis had achieved a goal cherished since his arrival in California some seven years earlier. He had made the change from immaturity to proficiency in business matters. In the interim he had not only tasted success, but had earned enough to buy his way into an established firm. Ahead lay prospects of greater profits and of winning further prominence in both Hawaii and California.

[18]Davis to Paty & Co., Dec. 22, 30, 31, 1845, SL; Paty & Co. to Davis, Dec. 22, 30, 31, 1845, SL; R. G. Davis to Davis, May 2, 1845, SL; Honolulu *Polynesian*, Dec. 17, 1845; Reynolds to Larkin, Feb. 14, 1846, LP.

Davis was justifiably excited and considered himself fortunate to be entering into association with men he already knew. His senior partner, Captain Eliab Grimes, an elderly and wealthy Honolulu merchant, had once hunted sea otter along the California coast with his father. Robert Grimes Davis, William's brother, was named after him and William had transacted business for Grimes in California.

At his uncle's Yerba Buena home William came to know Grimes intimately. During many wintry nights the temperamental but likable Whig engaged in political discussions in Spear's parlor and as he unwound himself what started out to be a calm discussion grew into a torrent of oratory sometimes lasting through an entire evening. Grimes's monologues drew quite an audience especially when he recounted with pride the story of his service against the British in the War of 1812. Another of his favorite topics was the future annexation of California by the United States, a course which he approved.

A favorite after-dinner sport of William and his uncle was to try to get Grimes to serve them a drink from the cache he carried with him. Only a good story could arouse the captain's humor sufficiently to get him to open his widely renowned wooden liquor case. Grimes often reacted to Yerba Buena's ordinary table talk by "looking sternly over his spectacles at the narrator," usually following the recital of a dull tale by growling "some discouraging epithet."

Though brusque and opinionated Grimes was essentially a kind man well liked both in Hawaii and California. In the Sacramento Valley he was awarded a large land grant by California's Mexican government and he stocked his rancho with 20,000 cattle. Grimes proved as meticulous in its management as he was in the trading firm which he and his nephew, Hiram, operated together. The captain sometimes lived at the ranch but more often was at Yerba Buena to take care of his trading activities. This, then, was the sort of man with whom William was joining forces.

Captain Grimes's nephew, Hiram, did not stand nearly so high in Davis's regard as his uncle. In fact, William soon came to dislike this young taskmaster. The new partners' plan of operation was to keep Hiram in Honolulu at the main headquarters of their firm; Captain Grimes was to alternate between managing his ranch and running a Yerba Buena depot and store; and William was to conduct their business at sea from Honolulu to Yerba Buena and along the California shore.

For their new enterprise the partners purchased the English brig *Euphemia* once used in the China trade. Old man Grimes, who had considerable influence with Robert Crichton Wyllie the Hawaiian King's Minister of Foreign Affairs, registered the vessel under the Hawaiian flag at Honolulu. Hiram assembled a $60,000 cargo calculated to sell handsomely on the coast. Though the total amount necessary to enter into the partnership absorbed most of his savings, Davis confidently went about the job of readying the new vessel for sea. Because he was already so well known in California his partners agreed that the *Euphemia's* operations should be transacted in the name of William Heath Davis. As a result their Hawaiian friends, who came down to Honolulu's harbor to help load the *Euphemia*, believed that Davis owned the greater share of the ship. This impression he was perfectly content to encourage.

Late in February 1846 the new entrepreneur gave orders to the *Euphemia's* master to weigh anchor and the box-like ship sailed from Honolulu on the first of many similar voyages.[1] The *Euphemia* was soon out of sight of land and in the heavy seas that characterized the passage of ships bound from Honolulu to the mainland of North America. As the vessel sailed onward, with an occasional whale surfacing in the distance, Davis smoked his

[1]Honolulu *Friend*, Mar. 2, 1846.

43

pipe in satisfaction and contemplated his new status. Bracing himself against the pitch and roll of the deck, he looked ahead with anticipation to sailing into Monterey as an independent trader.

On the last morning of March Davis heard his lookout from the crow's nest announce the sighting of land. He then supervised the ship's entry into a California port. The sails were furled, the anchor was lowered, and a salute to the Mexican flag flying above Monterey's Presidio was fired with a cannon borrowed from his old employer and new competitor, Captain Paty.

After Davis had registered his new status with General Castro, Monterey's *comandante general*, he diplomatically offered the general some kegs of scarce paint for his weather-beaten headquarters building. The "novice" made other gifts to lesser customs officials. To the collector of the port he gave a basket full of bottles of champagne, some sweet potatoes, and a few Hawaiian cocoanuts. Then, for a fee, Davis engaged American Consul Larkin to arrange clearance of the *Euphemia* for trading along the California coast.[2]

Following the custom of the country, the trader sent invitations to leading local merchants to visit his ship. He made sure they would arrive at precisely the time that Monterey's officialdom came aboard to examine the cargo. He knew that the festivities would distract the government authorities from their inspection and he outdid himself in providing "a handsome collation" of meats, fowls, jams, pies, cakes, fruits, and wines.

More important than all the food and presents he distributed were his preparations for handling the Monterey customs inspector. Davis hoped to keep the inspector from making anything like an adequate evaluation of the *Euphemia's* cargo, even though part of it was hidden, and he knew from past experience that he could take advantage of the fears and prejudices of that old and credulous official. When the inspector came abroad, Davis told him a long yarn about the number of scorpions the ship had acquired

[2]Monterey dockings of both the *Euphemia* and *Don Quixote* are listed in "Import-Duty Record Book," MS, n.d., Customs House, Monterey, Calif.; Davis to Larkin, Apr. 24, 1846, LP; Larkin to Davis, Apr. 28, 1846, in possession of H. F. Bruning, Palo Alto, Calif.

from its Honolulu cargo. During the warm passage from the islands, he explained, these had multiplied to an extraordinary degree. When he called the attention of the inspector to some specimens of the poisonous insects, that official lost all interest in going below deck to examine the cargo and assessed it at only a fraction of its dutiable value. Even so Davis paid $10,000 in duties to the Monterey Customs House.[3]

After clearing his cargo through customs Davis obtained permission to build an eighty-foot table in the Customs House on which to display his wares.[4] This was a real sales innovation and it pleased the *Californios* who liked buying their goods within the Customs House instead of clambering aboard slippery and dirty ships like the *Euphemia*. Davis was gratified to see many friends among those who drifted down toward the waterfront to buy his goods and experienced little difficulty in selling almost his entire cargo.

Eliab Grimes, who had come from Yerba Buena to supervise the activities of his new partner, was amazed at the young man's mastery of the techniques of selling. Previously fretful about this first venture, Grimes was pleased to observe William's calmness and his ability to obtain high prices. His immediate success in manipulating the captain's investment in their enterprise quickly earned him a drink from Grimes's liquor case—even without the telling of a story.

Far different from Eliab Grimes's reaction to Davis's success would be that of his other partner, the suspicious Hiram. In a parting letter of instruction he had warned the young super-cargo: "I wish to impress deeply upon your mind, not to smuggle my goods on the coast of California." Ignoring these instructions Davis, prior to his landing at Monterey, had made a side trip to San Nicholas Island. In caching there part of the *Euphemia's* most dutiable goods, he had followed the practice of Abel Stearns and of many others who used southern California's channel islands for hiding supplies from Monterey's customs authorities. Davis, incidentally, omitted all mention in his printed writings

[3]Pablo de la Guerra to Davis, Apr. 7, 1846, SL; *75 Years*, pp. 262-63.

[4]*75 Years*, pp. 262, 264. Mrs. Mary Greene, Curator of the Monterey Customs House, states that Davis exaggerated the table's length.

of his excursion southward; yet this detour had made his first trip to California a resounding success.[5]

After later retrieving his hidden cargo Davis wrote Hiram concerning certain perplexing shortages. He even accused him of making some purposeful "errors in the weight of the coffee. Yea, and in some other things" that his partner was supposed to have loaded aboard the *Euphemia*. Davis argued that when competing against a Henry Mellus, the efficient supercargo of the vessel *Barnstable*, such miscalculations became especially serious handicaps. Successful trading, after all, required having quantities of salable supplies below decks, unloading them quickly, and turning over such goods rapidly, thus assuring flexibility of operations. With misgivings about meeting all the requirements needed for such trading on a large scale, Davis completed his selling at Santa Cruz. From there he rode overland by horse through the mustard toward Yerba Buena, while the *Euphemia* made her way north by sea.[6]

Upon arriving home Davis had to procure quarters for the new firm since he could no longer use Paty & Company's adobe. He rented his uncle's store until he and Eliab Grimes could build one of their own on land recently purchased by Davis near the waterfront. From Spear's remaining supply of goods he chose the more salable items to load on the *Euphemia* for the next leg of her journey to the southern leeward ports. For cousin William Goodwin Dana at Nipomo he packed aboard such items from Honolulu as calico prints, axes, and cherry cordial and for John Temple at Los Angeles an assortment of velvet vests, castor oil, and essence of peppermint. For various other southern California merchants he prepared invoices and remittances collected in the north. In addition, Davis went through the large accumulation of orders which Eliab Grimes had assembled for him. He was amused at a bizarre request from Hawaii for ten female deer and two males for breeding purposes. "The more you send," a cus-

[5]"The First Voyage of the Euphemia and Her Evasion of Revenue," Huntington MS. DA 2(111) gives details of Davis's side trip; Cleland, *Cattle*, p. 188, describes Stearns's smuggling.

[6]Grimes to Davis, Feb. 21, 1846, SL. A list of the ship's manifest on the *Euphemia's* first voyage, dated Mar. 30, 1846, is among the Bancroft Library MSS; Davis to E. & H. Grimes, Apr. 17, 1846, "Davis Letterbook," SL.

tomer pointed out, "the quicker you can have a deer or stag hunt."[7]

Although busy opening the new business and taking orders for the future delivery of supplies, Davis was above all concerned over the absence of the *Euphemia*. There were storms all along the coast and the ship was long overdue at Yerba Buena. When she had been missing eleven days, he wrote Larkin that "if she is not in by tomorrow evening, I shall give up seeing her again." Much to his relief the brig's sails finally appeared over Yerba Buena's horizon.

Almost immediately Davis began to load her for the voyage. Before sailing south, Davis took the *Euphemia* to Sausalito across San Francisco Bay. There she picked up fresh water and quantities of flour from Spear's new rancho plus bags of the dirty and rancid tallow which Davis marketed, at no profit to himself, out of affection for his uncle. Davis also thoughtfully delivered to his Aunt Jane several barrels of Hawaiian *poi* and some boxes of salted island fish.

These Hawaiian foods, plus champagne and *aguardiente*, helped make reunions with the Spears truly gala occasions. At Sausalito Davis invited aboard the *Euphemia*, in addition to his uncle, a large number of men who celebrated the completion of his first independent voyage. In order to keep his competitors confused he had to be especially careful not to give away the *Euphemia's* next destination. The quantities of alcohol consumed scarcely helped him to keep his secret, for all hands aboard toasted his success over and over again and the celebration left him reeling from its effects. His uncle was surely the proudest of all who raised their glasses to join in the many toasts to his continued good fortune.

There were members of the opposite sex whose interest Davis also captured during this stay on San Francisco Bay. On the day after his stag celebration Jane Spear boarded the *Euphemia* with María Jesús Estudillo. He had seen her only occasionally since that day in 1842 when they had met at Larkin's in Monterey. William gave the young lady some carefully selected "white

[7]Davis to Larkin, May 6, 1846, SL.

47

silk handkerchiefs and fancy goods" as a demonstration of his fondness for her. He was now a merchant in his own right and could afford to entertain a member of the noted Estudillo family of San Leandro in the proper manner. William would be seeing more of their favorite daughter.

With his entertaining over all too soon, Davis headed the *Euphemia* out of the Golden Gate and just a month after she had first entered Monterey the ship again put in at that harbor. She went on during the next several weeks to make other landfalls at Santa Barbara and San Diego. Once Davis disposed of most of his goods, he gave orders to steer the ship back to Yerba Buena. He was anxious to outfit her for a trip to Oahu where Hiram Grimes had another cargo waiting. But before the *Euphemia* could return to Yerba Buena, political events of great consequence were to prevent Davis from going to Honolulu.[8]

During the month or more that the *Euphemia* had taken to make the rounds of the province's leeward ports, agitation for California's acquisition had developed in the East. The future status of California had long been a matter of public discussion and the American press, particularly James Gordon Bennett's New York *Herald*, had been urging readers to exert pressure upon their congressmen to secure the region for the United States. What Davis and his fellow Americans in the remote province of California could scarcely be expected to understand was that with her government in the hands of a weak Mexican bureaucracy a power vacuum had been created. As a result of the jockeying for position there of various nations, he and his compatriots were about to become enmeshed in a chain of events which culminated in American possession of the Pacific West.

Over the years Davis had noticed a growing number of English ships along the coast and he half believed that if California were ever lost to a foreign power it would be to England. He and his crew, in fact, talked about that hazard as they sailed up the coast to Monterey.

The residence there of settlers like Davis had encouraged a growing national sentiment for annexation and the election of President James K. Polk on an anti-British, pro-expansion plat-

[8]Davis to Larkin, May 12, 1846, LP.

form intensified interest in acquiring that territory. After failing to buy the province from Mexico, Polk instructed his confidential agent in California, Thomas Oliver Larkin, discreetly to persuade the *Californios* to break away from Mexico. Larkin contacted his friend Davis, as well as other Yankees, in an effort to line them up on the American side. To Davis he wrote:

Should there be a war you may find a good chance for employ for your vessel being under a neutral flag. . . . You may depend on my giving your Brig something to do.[9]

Larkin was soon able to keep his promise for war was declared between the United States and Mexico and Commodore John Drake Sloat, commander of United States naval forces in the Pacific, occupied Monterey. Davis and his men, of course, were unaware of this dramatic event. When the *Euphemia* shortened sail to round Point Pinos and entered the harbor of Monterey, all hands were amazed to see a resplendent American flag flying above the customs house! For foreign traders like Davis, that building was the center, indeed the very symbol of Mexico's governmental jurisdiction.

Davis soon learned that, unlike the premature flag-raising in 1842, a fully authorized naval force this time had taken over California's capital and that several warships, including the sixty-four-gun frigate *Savannah*, lay anchored in the harbor. More important, he learned that the United States was already at war with Mexico. He thereafter never ceased to boast that his brig was the first commercial vessel to enter Monterey following the raising of the American flag on July 7, 1846, and that he had been met at the Monterey waterfront by American Consul Larkin who introduced him to Commodore Sloat.[10]

[9]Larkin to Davis, Apr. 28, 1846, in possession of H. F. Bruning, Palo Alto, Calif.; other letters that give a picture of this particularly critical period are Davis to Larkin, May 6, 1846, LP, and Davis to Thomas Russom, Apr. 25, 1846, "Davis Letterbook," SL.

[10]*75 Years*, p. 266; Davis to Fitch, July 27, 1846, "Davis Letterbook," SL. One writer has suggested that it was unusual that Sloat, a diffident man, should have joined Larkin at the waterfront in welcoming so youthful a trader as Davis. This critic, Major Edwin A. Sherman, was, however, such a devotee of Sloat that he denounced the historian Hubert Howe Bancroft and Davis too for questioning his hero's role in the conquest of California. See Sherman, *The Life of the Late Rear-Admiral John Drake Sloat* . . . (Oakland, 1902), pp. 10-18.

Sloat was soon relieved by a more vigorous commander, Commodore Robert F. Stockton, who hoped for an orderly transition from Mexican to American control. At the same time Stockton believed in building up his forces to prepare for any eventuality and Davis found himself in the right place at the right time to take advantage of wartime conditions at Monterey. Large purchases of goods by Stockton's sailors and marines so depleted his merchandise that he sent the *Euphemia* to Honolulu for supplies. With her cargo of lumber and other local products Davis dispatched to Hiram Grimes $1,800 in gold and numerous "pursers bills" for goods already furnished the United States Navy. Almost overnight he became a significant military supplier.

After the *Euphemia* departed for Hawaii Davis rode north to Yerba Buena on horseback. As he cantered over the hills sloping down toward that village so soon to become a large city, he moved toward a scene similar to that at Monterey and was thrilled again to see the American flag flying over the Yerba Buena Presidio and raised above the *U.S.S. Portsmouth*. Captain John B. Montgomery, commander of the vessel, invited aboard Davis and other members of the small community of Americans who would shape the future San Francisco. As he sat at the captain's table, surrounded by the blue uniforms that signified American control of California, Davis saw that in a political as well as in a commercial sense, he and the other Americans in California had made a place for themselves within the expanding American empire. For the first time ships and men had been sent to protect them and to foster their well-being.

With the evidence of Yankee power everywhere at hand, Yerba Buena's Americans soon held a municipal election to replace Mexico's local officials. Chosen to be the election inspector, Davis tallied the hundred-odd votes deposited in the community's ballot box which was, quite typically, a crate recently used to ship lemon syrup around the Horn. In that early period of American control over California political success came easily to those who wished it because of the sparsity of Americans in California; had Davis possessed political ambitions, he might have seized the opportunity to cast his hat into the political arena.

But his major interest was in commerce and he returned to merchandising where he felt more confident.

With other leading local citizens he proudly greeted Commodore Stockton when he arrived at Yerba Buena to inspect Captain Montgomery's operations. Davis, Captain Grimes, and a coterie of Americans accepted the commodore's invitation to join in the victory parade that rode from the waterfront to the presidio near the tip of the peninsula. Such festivities were unfortunately soon marred by a revolt in southern California against the American garrison and Stockton immediately headed south. Before he left he asked Davis to purchase as many pistols and rifles as he could secure from the local populace. The trader bought from the Mormon, Samuel Brannan, many scarce weapons which he later sold in the south to Stockton and to John C. Frémont, the naturalist-explorer-soldier whose expedition became involved in the conquest of California.[11]

Davis found that now he had almost too many customers. In addition to the demands of the military for supplies, hundreds of people in the interior had become dependent upon merchants like himself for services and provisions. And they became disgruntled whenever he did not fulfill their expectations. Once the annoyed German founder of New Mecklenberg (Marysville), Theodor Cordua, angrily demanded an explanation of Davis's failure to return some watches which he had taken to Hawaii to be repaired three years before! He even charged that Davis's inefficiency was due to inebriation, an assertion which the trader resented. To placate such customers, late in 1846, Davis journeyed inland to bring them supplies. On that trip he traded with Sutter again and once more heard Sutter's familiar lament: "I am sorry you are not better disposed toward me."[12] But Davis personally was not hostile toward Sutter despite his irritating business methods.

[11]James H. Gleason to Davis, Oct. 16, 1846 and H. Grimes to Davis, June 26, 1846, SL; for one analysis of Frémont's colorful career see Allan Nevins, *Frémont, Pathmarker of the West* (New York, 1939).

[12]Sutter to Davis, Aug. 14, 1846, in possession of H. F. Bruning, Palo Alto, Calif.; Cordua to Davis, July 5, 1846, SL, and Nov. 28, 1842, UCLA. See "The Memoirs of Theodor Cordua, the Pioneer of New Mecklenburg in the Sacramento Valley," ed. and trans. Erwin G. Gudde, *Calif. Hist. Soc. Quarterly*, XII (1933), 281-311.

Back at Yerba Buena Davis sensed the economic future of its deepwater harbor which would eventually become California's maritime and customs center. In a letter to Fitch, he gave "thanks to God" that "the stars and stripes" would "now fly forever" over America's western gate. "Now my friend hurry yourself up to Yerba Buena," he counseled, "for this is going to be the paradise of California."[13] Continuing to boast, Davis claimed that his *Euphemia* was the first ship to pay American duties at Yerba Buena. He wisely asked Hiram Grimes for dozens of cases of New England rum, now in real demand among the American bluejackets, and quickly resold each gallon, costing $1 in Honolulu, at $3 to $5. Davis's cargo of 200 barrels of flour, 8,000 pounds of coffee, 30,000 pounds of sugar, and such luxuries as "segars," snuff, and even collar buttons was bought up rapidly.

He also made a sizable profit in southern California when he chartered the ship *Brooklyn* (on which Samuel Brannan's company of Mormons had recently arrived) and sent her with barley and other supplies to Commodore Stockton. Because military demands in the south assured sufficient business for numerous vessels, he welcomed the return of the *Euphemia* to California waters from Hawaii. But the more he employed this ship, the more Davis came to consider her an inefficient and basically unsound craft. As she could carry only 75,000 feet of lumber and shingles to Hawaii, he suggested to Hiram Grimes that they purchase a larger vessel. This proposal was not favorably received by his partner and Davis's temper rose.

Despite the reduction of their profits by continual bickering with Hiram, Davis was in the midst of flush times in California. To exploit the opportunities of the moment he stocked the *Euphemia* for trading nearer the "seat of the war." In her cargo intended for the military in southern California, he included boots and brogans, tea and coffee, liquors and wines, sugar and flour, plus ale and porter. Davis counted upon Frémont's forces, then heading south for battle, to clear the path for him. In a letter to a friend he wrote:

[13] July 27, 1846, "Davis Letterbook," SL.

I place great confidence in being able to trade at Santa Barbara, on my way down, from the fact that Col. Fremont has left here with a force of four hundred mounted men. . . . There is a very strong possibility that he will restore the American flag and make such arrangements as will be safe for us to visit, and . . . trade at the places he reaches in advance of us. . . .[14]

Upon his arrival at Santa Barbara Davis found that his predictions were correct. The military had indeed cleared out unfriendly Mexicans and American purchases induced an even freer circulation of money than in northern California. At the formerly sleepy pueblo Davis's clerks unloaded casks of rum, hogsheads of dried beans, and crates of woolens for the military.

Davis and other traders were so busy filling orders that they almost left out of their plans a most important participant in California's conquest—Frémont. The "Pathfinder" was at this time advancing upon the Mexican forces further south. Although Davis counted on Frémont's force to make his trading activities safer, he had not inquired as to whether the commander needed supplies. As he prepared to sail southward from Santa Barbara, Davis heard from the "Pathfinder." He was visited by three officers from Frémont's battalion while at the de la Guerra home who told him that their leader wanted him to come to their camp outside Santa Barbara.

Frémont had bivouacked there to give his battered force a rest. Drenched by the rain Davis made his way through large puddles of water to the muddy campsite. When told of Frémont's need for supplies, he was torn between patriotism and self-interest —Frémont had no cash. Davis later stated, "While I wanted to assist the government and to do everything I could toward making the men under Frémont comfortable, at the same time I did not care to become his creditor."

But the shrewd New Englander in Davis was vanquished by his generous Hawaiian background. Moved by the ragged condition of the "Pathfinder's" forces, the young trader agreed to give the almost equally young commander such supplies as he requested. As no one knew what kind of resistance the Mexicans might offer his men further south, Davis extended credit to

[14]Ibid., Dec. 14, 1846.

Frémont for some $6,000 worth of goods. To the quantities of coffee, flour and tea which he gave the "Pathfinder," he added 15,000 percussion caps, numerous barrels of pig lead for bullets, and 10,000 pounds of brown sugar. This precious merchandise could have been sold to the navy either for cash or redeemable vouchers, but Davis decided, especially after Frémont promised to pay within six weeks, that he needed these supplies more than Stockton. After unloading the goods, Davis sailed for his next port of call, San Diego.[15]

At this southernmost of California's harbors he renewed his acquaintance with Stockton. The Commodore was most cordial and not only included Davis among those invited aboard his flagship, but promptly and personally handled a payment of some $4,000 to him for supplies delivered to the navy. Stockton was thereafter his personal hero of the conquest of California.[16]

At San Diego Davis met an old but friendly rival, Henry F. Teschemacher, of the Boston bark *Tasso*. Like Davis, he wanted to travel toward Los Angeles where the last of the Mexican forces were reputedly deployed. After trading at San Diego, Davis and his friend heard the news that Frémont had received the surrender of these forces on January 13, 1847, just outside Los Angeles. Davis and Teschemacher immediately struck out overland on horseback for that pueblo and ordered their vessels to proceed northward to the roadstead of San Pedro which served as the harbor for Los Angeles. On the way the pair stopped at Rancho Santa Ana, owned by a lady whom Davis termed the "fascinating widow of Don Tomás Yorba." Davis, always taken by Doña Vicenta's beauty, knew how to praise that quality and, on this trip alone, he obtained from her an order for some $3,000 worth of supplies.

After resting at Doña Vicenta's rancho, Davis and Tesche-

[15]Part of the documentation of the Frémont-Davis relationship is in: *75 Years*, pp. 274-77; R. M. Sherman to Davis, Jan. 18, 1847, and Davis to Henry King, Feb. 11, 1847, "Davis Letterbook," SL. See also U. S. Congress, "Proceedings of the Court Martial In The Trial of Lieutenant Colonel Fremont," *Senate Exec. Doc. No. 33* (Washington, 1847), pp. 6-7; Vallejo Document No. 254, XXXIV (n.d.), BL.

[16]At San Diego Davis visited General Stephen W. Kearny's dragoons wounded at the Battle of San Pasqual. Fitch to Davis, June 22, 27, 1846, SL, and Sept. 15, 1846, UCLA; San Francisco *Call*, Mar. 10, 1877.

macher prepared for the next leg of their trip. On fresh horses obtained from her, they forded the swollen Santa Ana and San Gabriel rivers and threaded their way over a deeply rutted road toward Los Angeles. On its outskirts the two were met by friends who regaled them with hot punch. The discomforts of their trip were forgotten after an enjoyable meal provided by Doña Arcadia, Don Abel's wife. Davis was always partial to her husband, a plain-spoken and ugly man affectionately called "Horseface" behind his back.

Davis had come to Los Angeles primarily to call upon Frémont who had recently been appointed American Governor of California. Since the war was now over he expected Frémont to settle the accounts due him. When he was, instead, put off by subordinates Davis was offended. He thought he was at least entitled to courteous treatment after his recent valuable assistance. "If he was not prepared to redeem his promise, he could at least have said so in a fair, square, and manly way," the trader later wrote. Part of his claim against Frémont, amounting to over $5,000, remained unsettled.[17]

Once convinced that Frémont had no immediate intention of paying his obligations, Davis ordered the *Euphemia* north to Yerba Buena. He decided to continue the horseback trip with Teschemacher to see how his many ranchero friends had fared during the conquest and to take their orders for future delivery of goods. After resting at such places as cousin William Goodwin Dana's Rancho Nipomo, the supposedly rival merchants camped many nights together under open, peaceful skies. Both gave thanks to God that the war was over and that none of their friends on either side had been seriously injured.

Upon his return to Yerba Buena, Davis was embarrassed to learn that one of his assistants had been arrested by the military

[17]In U.S. Congress, "Report of the Secretary of War . . . ," *Senate Exec. Doc. No. 8* (Washington, 1854), pp. 6, 7, 15, Davis is a claimant for a total of $3,167.02 for ordnance stores, subsistence, horses, and clothing supplied Frémont. After Davis dissolved his partnership with the Grimeses in 1848, the Frémont account surrendered to them still remained unpaid. The settlement of such "California claims" against the American military, in fact, went on for years. William Goodwin Dana, however, refused to accept payment for supplies furnished Frémont. See H. Grimes to Davis, Dec. 23, 1849, Mar. 17, May 20, 1857, Jan. 20, 1858, Oct. 6, 1859, UCLA.

authorities. This eccentric individual, "Philosopher" Charles E. Pickett, was confined in Davis's store which had been boarded up by Commodore Joseph Hull who now commanded American naval forces in the north. Hull had taken strong exception to certain of "Philosopher" Pickett's criticisms of the military and had ordered him jailed. Davis was to experience other exasperating moments over his employment of Pickett, one of the West's most colorful characters.[18]

After obtaining Pickett's release, Davis straightened out other complications. His store accounts and correspondence had not only been neglected during the conquest period, but contacts with regular customers needed to be restored. With peace now the condition that guided his future course, he sent into the field two clerks, Josiah Belden and R. M. Sherman, with orders to collect from delinquent patrons and to deliver supplies recently ordered by rancheros. Belden and Sherman used a launch to cross the bay and when they went to isolated areas employed Kanaka or Indian helpers. Even though the launch sometimes proved precarious in a storm, it became their symbol of paid bills. Without the launch, supplies would never have reached many trappers, miners, and rancheros nor could their bills have been collected. "Without the launch," Davis once reminded his clerks, "we are done up."[19]

Relatives in Hawaii had been kept informed of the great success in military trading that Davis had enjoyed. His association with the commander of American naval forces in the Pacific, his appointment as a California election inspector, and his huge orders for supplies from his jealous partner, Hiram Grimes, were all subjects of discussion at Honolulu. William's mother and brother were also pleased to learn that he had been appointed the agent of the newspaper *Californian* in Hawaii. When Davis's profitable "war trading" ended in March 1847, his accounts were etched in black. That month he took over $20,000 in

[18]*75 Years*, p. 275; Lawrence Clark Powell, *Philosopher Pickett* . . . (Berkeley, 1942), pp. 21-24, 26, 28-29, 31-32, 124.

[19]Belden also represented Larkin while in charge of Davis's business. He left Davis's employ in 1848 to open a store for Mellus & Howard at San Jose and became the city's first American mayor.

coin and United States Navy vouchers on the *Euphemia* to Hiram Grimes in Honolulu. He was justifiably proud of these accomplishments.

Originally he had not planned to go to Honolulu but shortly before the *Euphemia* left he heard that his mother was seriously ill. He decided to sail at once. As Captain Grimes was in Hawaii, Davis had to make arrangements to leave his business in good hands. He had learned how foolish it was to trust unreliables like Pickett with his business affairs. Although California was under the military control of his own countrymen Davis paradoxically distrusted many of the gringo drifters who were making their appearance at Yerba Buena. He still had faith in the local rancheros but not in some of the Yankees he had recently encountered. Attached to a letter of instructions left by Davis with his clerks as he departed for Honolulu, was a restricted list of persons whom he deemed good credit risks. He warned them also to "keep a bright eye" on the "damnable opposition" posed by new merchants like Ward & Smith who were cutting sugar prices to ten cents a pound when the going rate was sixteen. Davis cautioned his employees to "be very guarded" and to keep accounts to themselves. He even wanted to give everyone the impression "that we are doing a small business."

In addition to his clerks, Davis left at Yerba Buena "two boys" and a cooper whom he admonished "to keep busily employed" either in delivering goods, cutting firewood, or planting vegetables behind the store. Davis warned that "while cooking their own victuals," these employees must, furthermore, not waste his food. He even left instructions about how María Jesús Estudillo, his future fiancee, should be treated: "Please pay all gentility," he urged. But he also warned, "be careful how far you attempt to take my place in this gentility."[20]

At Honolulu neither his presence nor all the money Davis had amassed could save his mother from dying only a few days after his arrival. The Hawaiian newspaper, the *Friend*, was most

[20]Davis to Sherman, Nov. 6, 1846, "Davis Letterbook," SL; see also Davis to M. J. Davis, Mar. 28, 1847, UCLA; Sherman to Davis, June 26, 1847, SL and Jan. 18, 1847, UCLA.

impressed by her large, native-language funeral. Davis spoke of his loss as "the first real sorrow I ever experienced, a blow from which it will take a long time to recover."[21] Despite his grief he quickly made plans to leave Honolulu. His mother's death had reminded him more than ever of his firm attachment to California.

Upon his return Davis saw many signs that indicated how the province had already changed from its former sleepy Arcadian status. The Americanization of the Far West had quickly made basic political and economic alterations necessary. As a result Davis sensed a rigidity in the air almost alien to the atmosphere he had known before. Just how the intrusion of a new social order would affect his future was still a matter of uncertainty. Yet, whenever he looked back upon California's conquest by the Americans, Davis remembered himself as an advocate of United States acquisition. He gathered satisfaction also from the way in which the conquest had officially substituted members of his own nationality for the *Californios* in a land where Americans were previously considered foreigners. The conquest period had meant a virtual trebling of his profits. Furthermore Yerba Buena had supplanted Monterey as California's most important center. Still confident about its future, he fortunately bought parcels of land before the rush for town lots occurred following the conquest era. For these and other reasons Davis counted himself lucky to have achieved, at his age, the high degree of success which the Americanization of California encouraged.

[21]*75 Years*, p. 293; Honolulu *Friend*, May 1, 1847; A. B. Thompson to Davis, July 16, 30, 1846, SL; Davis to Fitch, July 27, 1846, "Davis Letterbook," SL; Davis to E. Grimes, May 16, 1847, SL; "Glimpses," 335-54.

T HE CONQUEST OF California transformed Davis's way of life and modified the society in which he had reached maturity. Perhaps the major economic change accompanying Americanization of the province was the termination of the hide and tallow trade. Even before the conquest period was over the trading of hides became a comparatively petty operation because of the high prices paid rancheros for beef by American forces. Davis realized that the pastoral era was about to give way to a new order and expanded his activities to keep step with California's changing environment.

He had not only gained confidence as a trader but had amassed capital during the conquest and thought he was ready to undertake new and larger transactions. Americans arriving at San Francisco stimulated him by their talk of the large speculations common in the East. Davis knew that San Francisco needed new wharves to accommodate ships anchoring at that port as well as adequate docking facilities at tiny Loma Alta Cove, which was still the city's only harbor. He persuaded his senior partner, Eliab Grimes, to join him in a plan to build docks. They thus became San Francisco's first wharf speculators and in 1846 Larkin joined their association. The three men became the main partners in an organization called the Yerba Buena Wharf Company, and collected a subscribed capital of $10,000. Larkin's biographer calls theirs the first planned corporation in California.[1]

[1]Underhill, *Cowhides*, pp. 135-36; R. Semple to Davis, Oct. 9, 1846, in *75 Years*, p. 117; Charles M. Weber to Davis, Oct. 15, 1846, UCLA; George W. Bellamy to Davis, Oct. 15, 1846, SL; T. H. Green to Davis, Oct. 26, 1846, SL.

In a burst of energy the trio drew up plans for their project. But before they could proceed, Davis had to secure the permission of California's military governor, who was still in command of most civil affairs. In petitioning "His Excellency, Robert F. Stockton, Governor and Commander in Chief of California," for a grant of land some fifty feet wide, the partners claimed that local merchants were greatly inconvenienced because traders still had to land their cargoes on open beaches where they were at the mercy of damaging winds and blowing sand. Despite the strong case made by Davis and his associates the military government refused their petition for land running out into the bay's channel and San Francisco was consequently denied its first wharf.[2]

Undaunted by their failure, Davis and Grimes tried again under a different name. As treasurer of a new corporation known as the Central Wharf Company, Davis obtained permission of sorts from San Francisco's city council to build a dock for the city. But again he encountered trouble with the military. The wharf's construction was authorized only by the civilian officials of the new municipality and Stockton, as military governor, denounced the city council for exceeding its authority. Davis misinterpreted Stockton's rebuke as partly personal and resigned his position as treasurer of the new wharf company. To his partners he returned some $23,000 collected before the first stockholder's meeting. By losing his temper in this way Davis denied himself entry into that circle of men who came to control the San Francisco waterfront. Eventually not one but nine wharves were constructed and Davis was always reticent about discussing his unsuccessful attempts in the field.

At the Golden Gate his frustrations in wharf construction occurred while Davis was associated with Americans. In this and other instances when his operations depended upon his own countrymen, he sometimes emerged less successfully than when dealing with the native Californians. To them he was always affectionately referred to as "Don Guillermo," a friend and adviser, and a knowing interpreter of the oddities of Americans.

[2]Petition to Stockton by Davis, Larkin, and Grimes, Oct. 8, 1846, LP; Bancroft, *History*, V, 653n.

Davis not only continued to enjoy their respect but also their business.

Despite his growing interest in large speculations Davis still carried on the many smaller transactions with the natives on which his success had been built. His emporium supplied them with everything from yellow corn to turkey-red handkerchiefs. If a man wanted a flatiron, a cask of brandy, or a bag of shot, he could obtain them at the Davis place. As larger numbers of Americans appeared in California, Davis stocked more supplies characteristic of the American frontier elsewhere: axes, sole leather, wash basins, solder, balzarine, nails, and wire were among the goods he sent on mule and by boat to Americans in the backwoods. Among the newcomers whiskey and ale were far more popular than the wine and *aguardiente* formerly marketed in large quantities. A Yankee preference for white flour over the local corn meal called *harina* forced Davis to import it in larger quantities. Americans craved other items such as "long nine" cigars and favored cast-iron Boston cook stoves over California's brick ovens. Davis readily adjusted his trading to these new tastes.

Davis's place of business was more than a simple store. His clapboard shanty grew into one of San Francisco's busiest centers of social activity. Its redwood shingle, swinging in the wind over a sagging front porch, identified the spot where everyone in town came either to meet friends or to strike a bargain. On the building's roughhewn walls were plastered shipping posters announcing sailing dates as well as Davis's latest prices and his advertisements which had appeared in the *Californian* and *California Star*, the new San Francisco newspapers. Some indication of the scope of his business dealings may be gained from his notice in the *Star* for April 17, 1847, which offered for sale over 80,000 feet of Oregon lumber.

It was the lumber operation that ultimately led Davis into serious trouble with his partner, Hiram Grimes. Their relations were already strained by Hiram's insistence on sending him unsalable goods from Honolulu and only partly filled casks of brandy. On one occasion Davis wrote a six-page letter complaining about various goods "none of which I wrote for, and

61

none of which will sell here." Far from his usual calm self, in this letter he sarcastically rejected Grimes's explanation about having sent such cargo on the advice of persons in Honolulu.

If Mr. Reynolds, living there, knows better than I as to the amount of goods required here, then of course any advice from me on the subject is entirely uncalled for.

Davis reinforced this rebuke by sending back numerous items which he described as a "perfect drug here." He continually accused Hiram of shipping him goods at a higher cost than he paid for them in Honolulu and said that he could not "sanction" his "partners making a fortune out of a few goods and then turning them over to me to make another one for them."[3] Obviously a break with his partners was not far off.

Davis often pointed out to Hiram that with the passing of the conquest period, local consumers had postponed buying supplies in the hope of obtaining future reductions on eastern products. Such complaints had little effect on either of his partners. Despite the fact that they took him for granted, he continued to remonstrate loudly. When Hiram again exceeded Davis's order of goods by some $7,000, he threatened "to close the business as fast as I possibly can and carry it on my own."

His forthcoming break with Hiram Grimes was actually in part connected with California's growth, for as the bay region expanded in importance Davis felt an increased independence of the Honolulu market. By the end of 1847 Yerba Buena had become San Francisco, a community that boasted thirty-five whitewashed adobes and over 150 frame buildings. Davis knew that the once sleepy hamlet already had a concentration of commerce larger than any port on the West Coast and anticipated that the Golden Gate would become western America's main outlet for trade with the Orient. His partners did not share his enthusiasm. In 1847 when he first mentioned to Captain Grimes the idea of a trip to China to purchase Oriental luxuries for the California market Grimes was opposed to it. But Davis

[3]Davis to E. & H. Grimes, Nov. 17, 19, 1846 and Charles Brewer to Davis, Oct. 28, 1848, SL.

made covert plans for such a trip and warned his clerks not to "whisper a single word to anyone about the China voyage." To close friends he described his scheme as "in all human foresight pregnant with glorious success." Davis stubbornly continued to plan for this trip to the Orient and he even went so far as to cancel important lumber-hauling contracts to free the *Euphemia* for it. His partners, however, insisted on continuing the lumber trade.

The *Euphemia* regularly took on thousands of feet of boards at both Bodega Bay and San Jose which were sold by Hiram Grimes at lumber-hungry Honolulu. Davis, who believed the brig ill suited for such cargoes, kept her away from this traffic whenever possible. On one occasion he even forced his partners to charter the *Mount Vernon* to haul some 200,000 feet of lumber from the Columbia River. Actually they had good reason to be impressed by the lumber business; with San Francisco and numerous other communities now safely past the canvas stage, tons of timbers, planks, shingles, and bracings were everywhere needed. The construction of new cities depended upon a plentiful wood supply and the Grimeses meant to be among the major suppliers.

In addition to quarreling with them over the lumber trade, Davis was also angered by Hiram's resistance to his plan to put the *Euphemia* under American colors. He believed such action was imperative because of the Americanization of California. American customs charges on foreign ships had become so onerous that Davis even complained to California's new military governor and, against Hiram's wishes, he applied for a United States coasting license.[4]

Davis considered his customs worries only minor compared to the trouble with his partners. The frequent sickness of Captain Grimes served to sharpen already uneasy relations with Hiram because whenever the older Grimes came down with one of his "fever spells" the younger men ran the business. Davis wished that his future no longer depended upon associa-

[4]Davis to R. B. Mason, Oct. 22, 1847, SL; Joseph Lanman to Sherman, Jan. 11, 1848, Calif. Hist. Soc., San Francisco.

tion with Hiram. Disgusted with his conservatism, niggardliness, and lack of enthusiasm for new trading opportunities, Davis considered the possibility of asking his brother Robert to become his Hawaiian partner. But since he could not yet raise enough money to buy out the Grimeses, he was forced to continue his unpleasant business relationship with them.

About this time significant changes were taking place in the California business community. After the conquest of California another type of merchant arrived on the scene. With little respect for the earlier tradition of cooperation among traders, these new small firms—Ward & Smith, Dickson & Hay, Shelly & Norris, and Beasley & Company at San Francisco, Ruckel & Cooke at San Jose, and Scott & Boggs at Sonoma—practiced suicidal price cutting against which Davis naturally remonstrated. On one occasion he wrote:

I understand that Dicks and Hays [sic] are selling goods very low —oh what a pity that them chaps has come to San Francisco, but if fellows goes on in that way I shall do all in my power to put them down.[5]

Davis had quite different feelings for a firm like Howard & Mellus. William Davis Merry Howard, Davis's cousin, and his partner, Henry Mellus had bought out the Hudson's Bay Company property and on it built the first brick store in San Francisco. They established branches at Sacramento, San Jose, and Los Angeles and had become Davis's chief competitors; nevertheless this relationship was cordial.[6] He could trust a Howard or a Mellus, who resorted mainly to persistence and persuasion in trading. With them he had an understanding not to employ the sharp practices that eastern merchants brought into California. Davis and his friends, in fact, even accepted hides for each other's accounts from rancheros. Since California's hide and tallow days, when they had every incentive to band together,

[5]Davis to Sherman, Feb. 25, 1847, SL; Hubert Howe Bancroft, *California Pastoral, 1769-1848* (San Francisco, 1888), pp. 732-39 discusses some early San Francisco firms.

[6]Davis to Larkin, Apr. 24, 1846, LP; Starkey, Janion & Co. to E. & H. Grimes, May 3, 15, Sept. 6, Nov. 10, 1847, SL; H. Grimes to Davis, July 21, Aug. 7, 23, 1847, SL; Sherman to Sutter, Oct. 7, 1847, SL.

such traders had built up this spirit of cooperation. Their network included, in addition to Davis, Mellus, and Howard, men like Abel Stearns of Los Angeles who was fast becoming the "baron" of the southern cow counties. Because these contacts were social as well as economic, Davis never failed to bring them presents as symbols of his friendship. He usually brought dresses for the ladies of those traders at whose residence he called.[7]

As a bachelor in pre-Gold Rush San Francisco, Davis's business and social activities were inextricably interwoven. Now that Nathan Spear had gone inland to live, Davis spent considerable time with his cousin, Bill Howard, of whom he was especially fond. Howard would often rap on his door late at night to coax his more sober cousin into frolicking which sometimes continued until morning. Once during the conquest period, while the pair were out late tippling, they forgot the password requested by Stockton's marines who nightly patrolled the streets. When they were arrested for breaking the military curfew Howard, who according to Davis was "a capital mimic," turned their embarrassment into a farce which saw their jailers bursting with laughter. The two were quickly set free.

Despite these lighter moments, Davis generally worked hard. As California's American population grew he traveled more widely than ever. When he was off on trips, his clerks sometimes complained of a scarcity of foodstuffs. Of even more concern to them were the shortages of liquor which they insisted "we must have to treat friends." Whenever their favorite product, eastern bourbon whiskey, disappeared from the San Francisco market the clerks asked Davis to buy the brandy which he could readily procure at his various stops in the interior. He also sent them increasing quantities of cereals and garden vegetables since the growing population was creating a rising demand for wheat, fresh beans, corn, and peas. Although such perishables brought the highest prices at the bleak Russian

[7]*75 Years*, pp. 218-21, 246-49; Davis to Mellus, Oct. 24, 1846, Bancroft Library MSS; D. W. Alexander to Davis, Sept. 18, 1846, Feb. 8, 1847, "Davis Letterbook," SL; Davis to Stearns, Feb. 8, Sept. 3, 1847, Stearns Collection, Huntington Library.

settlements farther north, Davis ordinarily refused to venture into so remote a region. He preferred to deal with men who were his personal friends and would go to a great deal of trouble to help them. Once he hauled black sand—a most impractical cargo—over 2,000 miles from Honolulu to Benicia for his friend Larkin who was building a new city on the Carquinez Straits with his partner Robert Semple. With Larkin he engaged in various confidential transactions.[8]

Among the many activities in which Davis was involved a few were bound to be outside the natural orbit of his interests. For example he was once asked by the Reverend Richard Armstrong of Honolulu to distribute Christian tracts and testaments among the Hawaiians living in California. He performed this service primarily because he did not want to offend Armstrong who had helped bury his mother. The parson, however, went too far when he also requested Davis to ascertain the "leading moral character" among California's Hawaiian residents and to convince that person of the need for holding meetings with other brethren on the Sabbath. Davis informed him that such chores constituted too great a deviation from his normal activities.

Lately William's mind was fixed upon matters of more personal, indeed romantic, interest. As one Yankee friend after another married into California's local families he too began to think more seriously about taking a wife. Almost as if he did not trust his own judgment, he wrote his brother Robert seeking his advice about marrying María Jesús Estudillo with whom, he now admitted, he was "seriously in love." Robert, angry over William's failure to make him his partner, took this news ungraciously and irritated his brother by suggesting that a lady of such expensive tastes would "go into your purse." Despite the family's coolness toward his California señorita, William

[8]Larkin to Davis, Mar. 11, 1847 is reproduced, opposite p. 18 in 75 *Years*. See also Larkin to Davis, Mar. 13, 1847, SL; Davis to Larkin, Mar. 17, 18, 1847, Mar. 7, 1848, LP; Sherman to Larkin, Mar. 30, 1847, LP; Larkin in favor of Davis, Aug. 4, 1847, LP; Davis to Larkin, Nov. 6, 1847, "Davis Letterbook," SL; R. Semple to Larkin, Sept. 9, 1847, LP, states: "Mr. Davis has found one of the richest quicksilver mines in California." He may have been referring to a quicksilver mine of Spear's near Napa.

began to pay even more attention to the daughter of Don José Joaquín Estudillo of San Leandro.[9]

Her family was among the oldest in California. Years before, Davis's father had sold Boston goods to the Estudillos and was sufficiently impressed by their importance to include the name in his log book. As early as 1812 an Estudillo had been secretary of California's Council of State. Later María's father, Don José Joaquín, had distinguished himself as the pioneer alcalde of Yerba Buena. He and his wife, Juana, had reared four other daughters and six sons on the family lands. While they were not the largest California landlords, the territory of the northernmost Estudillos stretched along San Francisco Bay in narrow fingerlings from El Pinole in the Contra Costa region to San Leandro in present-day Alameda county.

The family possessed a remarkable reputation for hospitality; visiting hunters knew their lands not only as a veritable game preserve, but their household as a place where every effort was made to cater to comfort. The New England mariner, Captain "Webfoot" Phelps, was so impressed by his experiences at San Leandro that he wrote an account of his visit, which contains probably the only record in western historical annals of a goose hunt in which the game was lassoed. On this occasion, the Estudillos provided the old sea dog with a horse, and a boy, on still another mount, whose job it was to lasso and drag in such wounded birds as the hunter stalked.[10]

William always felt welcome whenever he visited the Estudillos of San Leandro, but some aspects of his courtship were trying. Since the *Californios* still upheld Old World formalities it was difficult for him to display his affection for María Jesús. Months transpired between William's first approach to the bride's mother in 1845 and his final letters to her father. William found the long wait for a wife tiresome, yet he respected local custom.

Knowing how much time it would take to convince the

[9]R. G. Davis to Davis, Aug. 19, 1847, UCLA; C. H. Pickett to Davis, May 13, 1847, SL; Powell, *Pickett*, pp. 29-33; Honolulu *Friend*, May 1, 1847.

[10]Phelps, *Fore and Aft*, pp. 341-48.

Estudillos that he was a proper son-in-law, for a time he deliberately avoided seeing María Jesús. His own anxiety and the envy of her unmarried sisters he hoped would thereby be forestalled. To secure the good will of Concepcíon, the eldest sister, Davis showered her with presents. As a consequence, María Jesús became confused about William's true affections and he had to reassure her that he was not interested in her sister.[11] An excellent portrayal of the courtship was written by one of his employees, a naïve clerk who later became a professor at Yale University:

This morning Mr. Davis returned from the other side of the Bay his 'ladylove' her sister and mother. The young ladies are elegant and even handsome, of medium size & figure, rather slender, black hair and eyes & light complexions . . . They have been since Sunday at midnight getting over, having high wind, & being driven far down the Bay. They suffered much from wet & cold, as it was a cold night & the spray dashed over the boat continually. They are unable to speak English & none of our household but Mr. Davis speaks Spanish.[12]

In quest of his future wife Davis enlisted the help of numerous mutual friends of the Estudillo family. Among these was William S. Hinckley, an old acquaintance of hide and tallow days, whom he sent to San Leandro on his behalf with the admonition to spare no possible compliments. The calculating suitor found that such "spontaneous visits" to the Estudillos helped immeasurably to convince them of his intentions.

By late 1846, Don José Joaquín Estudillo was addressing William as *"mi muy querido hijo."* And a "dearly beloved son" he was more than ready to become, for his impatience over the lengthy courtship was imposing a growing strain upon him. Yet the young couple had to wait for still more time to pass before they could even converse without others being present. Eventually the day came when Davis was allowed to announce his engagement. As a routine and almost accepted part of this

[11]Juana Martínez Estudillo to Davis, Dec. 5, 1846 and J. J. Estudillo to Davis, Aug. 21, Sept. 12, 1845, SL.

[12]Lyman, *Around the Horn*, pp. 210, 213.

formality he became a Catholic, like many other Yankees who married native California daughters.[13]

In November 1847, much to William's relief, the long-awaited wedding occurred, and the *California Star* and *Californian* reported the almost endless festivities. Since those early press notices, numerous writers have referred to the nuptials of William Heath Davis and María Jesús Estudillo as the most spectacular ever seen in California. Hers was still a wealthy family, anxious to make a correct impression in the Spanish tradition upon such neighbors as the Sotos, Castros, and Peraltas. They spared no expense.

Scores of richly clad relatives trekked from the interior to the bay to attend the celebration, traveling either by two-wheeled *carretas* or on horseback. A jet-black mount, adorned with gold and silver saddleware, brought the bride to Mission San Francisco de Asís where a crowd, including Davis's American friends, had assembled to witness the event. After the ceremony the festivities at Merrill's American House began with a magnificent dinner followed by champagne. Dining and wining and dancing lasted for three days until all were weary of merry-making. When the festivities ended, the bride and groom finally were allowed to settle down in a dwelling which William had recently built for María Jesús at Sacramento and Jackson streets. Even then his cousin, Howard, waggishly serenaded the tired couple with a band. Of this renewal of the celebration Davis later wrote:

When the band had played a number of airs on the piazza, we got up and dressed, opened the doors, and invited Howard and the musicians in . . . we had quite a party, champagne was freely opened . . .[14]

The nuptials of William and María Jesús constituted more than a wedding; the marriage also signified his fullest possible

[13]Hinckley to Davis, July 31, 1845, SL and Aug. 20, 1845, UCLA; J. J. Estudillo to Davis, Sept. 26, 1846, SL. See also Lieut. [Henry A.] Wise, U.S.N., *Los Gringos; or an inside view of Mexico and California with wanderings in Peru, Chili, and Polynesia* (New York, 1849), pp. 76-77.

[14]*75 Years*, p. 226; Bancroft, *History*, V, 685-86.

acceptance into the familial confidence of dozens of California's largest landholders. Families like the Estudillos still dominated the province's economy even though the many Americans invading the land of the dons would make this hegemony shortlived. Davis coupled his new status with the natives to his important American contacts and felt a greater security. This confidence was above all, however, based upon his union with a beautiful, olive-skinned bride who covered her dark hair with a lace mantilla and whose shoulders were warmed by a silk Canton shawl.

The new sense of security Davis felt eventually altered his outlook toward business and he came to the conclusion that his annoying partnership with the Grimeses must at all costs be terminated as quickly as possible. His returns from the trading agreement with them had been diminishing since the end of the conquest period, and he determined, if possible, even to precipitate a break in relations with them. His insistence upon undertaking long voyages, similar to the proposed China trip that his partners continually discouraged, further intensified the friction. Rumors were now trickling north from Peru of exceptional prices being paid for tallow, often amounting to as much as 100 per cent profit for California shippers. Davis, who thought that this might offer him a chance to revive the hide and tallow trade in a new form, argued a long time with his partners before they finally allowed him to prepare the *Euphemia* for a voyage to South America. But they made him assume responsibility for all losses incurred. On such terms he assembled a number of associates to help finance the purchase of large quantities of tallow; among them was Jean Jacques Vioget, whom Davis made master of the *Euphemia*. All the participants in this venture possessed high hopes for its success.

The trip, begun with such optimism, ended abruptly when the *Euphemia* struck a rocky crag near Monterey on her way to San Pedro to pick up the bulk of her cargo. Her master fortunately reached Monterey with her, but from there he reported to Davis that her crew, believing the leaking ship was not seaworthy, threatened to abandon it if she ever sailed again. Facing the wrath of his partners, Davis was mortified.

Captain Grimes now sternly ordered Davis to go to Monterey

and somehow get the brig afloat. By dint of considerable effort and after the use of quantities of rosin, tarpitch, and oakum, Davis readied the *Euphemia* for her return to San Francisco where she was careened, recaulked, and her bottom recoppered at his expense. Meanwhile his associates in the venture were literally left holding the tallow bags they had readied for the voyage to Peru.[15]

Disappointed by the first setback of his career and disheartened by what he considered the unreasonableness of his partners, Davis summed up his luck with the adage "Man proposes, God disposes!" Although his wife tried to console him, he believed his hopes of freeing himself from his association with the Grimeses to be dashed. The now unsalable tallow in which he had invested cost thousands of dollars. Furthermore, the time consumed in repairing the *Euphemia* kept her from gainful earnings.

But an element of surprise again lay ahead. While off once more with the *Euphemia* at Honolulu, Davis learned that gold had been discovered in California's Sierra. The ensuing Gold Rush would sweep him toward financial heights of which he had never dreamt.

[15]E. & H. Grimes to Davis, Feb. 1, 2, 3, 5, 1848, SL; M. J. Davis to Davis, Jan. 22, 23, Feb. 2, 1848, SL; Davis stayed at Monterey until Mar. 1848. See MS, "Monterey Consulate Archives," I, 43, BL; *Sandwich Island News* (Honolulu), Jan. 8, 1848.

CHAPTER VI

GOLD

C LOSELY FOLLOWING the American conquest of California, the Gold Rush was another epochal event in the life of William Heath Davis. The discovery of gold did not come completely as a surprise to him. Since the days when Spaniards first explored California's inland valleys, recurring Indian tales of gold in the interior had quietly reached the ears of some pioneers. Davis blamed Spain's padres and their secretiveness for postponing a gold rush which might have occurred earlier. Though he had once suggested to these Franciscans "that it would be better to make the matter known, to induce Americans and others to come" to California "to develop the country," the friars feared the repercussions of widespread immigration on their mission system.

The gold frenzy of 1848-1849, touched off by James Marshall's detection of some golden flakes in the tailrace of Sutter's American River sawmill, quickly erased any doubts about the existence of gold in the Sierra foothills. When Sam Brannan, Davis's fellow storekeeper at Sacramento, rushed to San Francisco, ran down its streets waving a medicine bottle full of yellow flakes, and cried out "Gold, Gold!" the peninsula was jolted into action. As Davis put it, many people immediately "hightailed" it out of town. By mid-summer of 1848 the city lay practically abandoned, most of its populace having already streaked to the mines. Among these "forty-eighters" were old time *Californios*, Indians, deserters from military garrisons, and scores of sailors who left behind a veritable armada of abandoned ships. All of them shouted for provisions. Dozens of their letters begging for supplies at any cost poured into Davis's store. No miner wanted to leave his gravel diggings in the Sierra stream beds even for an hour lest some new gold discovery materialize in his absence.[1]

Because of the scarcity of supplies at the mines Davis, as quickly as possible, sent out quantities of pots, pans, picks, shovels, axes, and crowbars. After his assistants lugged the merchandise inland over tortuous routes, across icy torrents, through mud and heavy brush, its cost soared. Prices skyrocketed beyond all reason. White flour rose to $800 a barrel, Kentucky Bourbon whiskey leaped overnight to $30 a quart; apples sold as high as $5 each, a dozen fresh eggs brought as much as $50 while tea and coffee cost from $300 to $400 a barrel. Davis sold butcher knives for $30 each, tin wash pans or bowls were cheap at $5; plain blankets were no less than $40, boots $100 a pair, medicine or pills $10 a dose, laudanum and other drugs $1 a drop. A twenty-five-foot plank cost $20, bulk lumber $500 a thousand feet, and Sam Brannan sold tacks for $192 a pound. Miners bought these supplies from wages considered to be high at $20 a day.

Heaps of gold piled up in San Francisco's stores and the most money was made right there by merchants like Davis. The traveling eastern journalist Bayard Taylor complained:

You enter a shop to buy something; the owner eyes you with perfect indifference, waiting for you to state your want; if you object to the price, you are at liberty to leave, for you need not expect to get it cheaper; he evidently cares little whether you buy it or not.[2]

Davis and other storekeepers were hounded by passengers arriving from all over the world who demanded supplies which

[1] Typical of the many letters Davis received requesting supplies from the mines are P. B. Reading to Davis, Dec. 10, 1848, UCLA, and G. D. Dickenson to Davis, May 1, 1849, SL.

[2] *Eldorado, or Adventures in the path of empire: comprising a voyage to California, via Panama* . . . (New York, 1850), I, 58-59; other descriptions of commercial conditions are in Caughey's *California*, pp. 291, 303 and his *Gold Is The Cornerstone* (Berkeley, 1948), pp. 17-38; Herbert Asbury, *The Barbary Coast; an informal history of the San Francisco underworld* (New York, 1947), pp. 11-13; Rodman W. Paul, *California Gold; the beginning of mining in the far West* (Cambridge, Mass., 1947), pp. 120, 349; Samuel C. Upham, *Notes of A Voyage To California via Cape Horn, together with scenes in El Dorado* . . . (Philadelphia, 1878), p. 259; Oscar Lewis, *Sea Routes to the Gold Fields; the migration by water to California in 1849-1852* (New York, 1949), p. 275.

had already disappeared. The year 1849 saw as many as twenty ships a day anchoring almost in front of his store. These were filled with gold-seeking Yankees, Chilenos, Kanakas, Chinese, and Frenchmen who were ferried to shore for $3 apiece. Connected with the excessive demands for supplies created by the arrival of the newcomers, was the decreased quantity of minted currency and surplus of raw gold. An important eastern shipper wrote that Mellus & Howard were

so surrounded with piles of gold dust & receive such enormous rents from their landed property, it is said 400 to $500,000 per annum, that they consider 10 to 12 thousand dollars for discharging a ship . . . a mere flea bite.[3]

As scarce silver disappeared from circulation, Davis and other merchants had a hard time finding enough coin to pay duties on incoming goods. Fortunately they were able to hit upon an awkward but workable plan with the port collector that solved the problem: they were allowed to pay duties by depositing gold dust with the collector in lieu of coin; later, when they had accumulated the necessary hard money, they could redeem the gold dust.[4]

Davis had great difficulty in disposing of the large amounts of gold dust he accumulated. He had either to ship it to the Philadelphia mint or to his eastern creditors; both methods were very expensive. "Beyond the Cape" the usual charge was 1½ per cent of the value of gold transported east, and a profitable return from dust shipments often depended upon having good eastern contacts.

Davis stumbled onto such a connection—developed by few California traders—in 1848 after he finally terminated his partnership with Hiram and Eliab Grimes. Except for the Gold Rush, Davis might never have been able to buy his way out of the partnership with the Grimeses and he might never have encountered the man who became his new partner. When he first met David Carter, this gentle, sandy-haired, young Boston

[3]Wm. Appleton & Co. to Mellus, Jan. 1, 1850, Dexter-Appleton Collection, XXXVII, Baker Library MS, Harvard University.

[4]75 Years, p. 309; S. H. Williams to Davis, Oct. 28, 1848, SL.

trader was marketing a trial cargo of goods which he had brought west. Davis became almost immediately indebted to him because Carter loaned him a sizable amount of scarce silver coinage. After Davis offered to market some undesirable vinegar and ship's bread for his new friend, the short-lived but highly successful firm of Davis & Carter was founded on August 21, 1848. Carter, who came to be liked by everyone, stood for a type of "business bigness" which Davis could never have achieved alone. The firm combined his western trading experience with Carter's eastern connections and greater capital. In a short time they practically doubled an original investment of several thousand dollars. With the scarce silver that Carter brought west Davis bought cargoes of highly desirable goods from Honolulu and received merchandise from Carter's jobber friends at the large Atlantic ports.[5]

By the end of 1848 Davis and Carter were exhilarated by their success. They spoke of increasing their business and of building a great firm together. They decided that Carter should travel east through Central America to obtain supplies and to carry back to the Philadelphia mint some $30,000 worth of surplus gold. Carter planned to purchase a new ship and cargo in the East and to return to San Francisco. He was also to bring back building materials for a fireproof store, so greatly needed in the city's tinderbox environs. Davis urged Carter to tell his Boston friends that he had been the first person to buy gold at San Francisco in June 1848. He later enjoyed repeating a tale about two miners who had stomped into his store with their "poke" tied in a doeskin bag, and in his *Seventy-Five Years in California* he boasted: "I was the first purchaser of the product of the mines."[6]

After Carter departed for the East, Davis turned to a variety

[5]Larkin to Davis & Carter, Oct. 11, 1848, Williams to Davis, Oct. 25, 1847, SL; Carter to Davis, Mar. 24, Apr. 27, 1848, SL; Davis to Carter, Apr. 13, 1848, UCLA; Davis to Carter, May 11, 1848, SL; San Francisco *Californian*, Sept. 2, 1848 (advertisement); Davis to Everett & Co., Aug. 23, 1848, SL.

[6]P. 309. Professor R. P. Bieber of Washington University has kindly furnished me with a reference from J. R. Snowden to David Carter, Dec. 11, 1848, in Letters Sent, U. S. Mint Records, Philadelphia (now National Archives) stating that Carter ultimately deposited $32,581.41 in gold at that mint.

of chores. Numerous persons now relied upon him to help them collect credits owed by the American military forces; newly arrived merchants depended on his advice regarding how best to market their goods; miners wrote him notes from vague mining addresses enclosing orders for supplies he could not possibly send or asking him to manage San Francisco property in the owner's absence. Even Captain Grimes, though supposedly angry with Davis, turned over his town rents and rancho lands for him to manage and departed for Hawaii to escape the ruckus of the rush. Fortunately the Grimeses were still willing to act as buyers for Davis on the Honolulu market and shipped him goods on the old brig *Euphemia* which he had bought from them.[7]

Because Davis formed temporary partnerships with various persons during the Gold Rush, his accounts were a veritable hodgepodge. To add to the confusion he had to accept local products in payment for manufactured goods, which meant keeping count of chickens, pigs, and cattle. Davis even became the owner of a herd of goats. Before the Gold Rush disturbed the local tranquillity, he had often fished and read on a quiet speck of land in San Francisco Bay (now known as Treasure Island) while crews of woodcutters gathered firewood. The islet's goats, belonging to his uncle and numbering several hundred, had kept Spear's crowded table supplied with tasty kid. Later a meat shortage, caused by the Gold Rush, led poachers to kill many of these goats. To keep from losing the remnants of Spear's depleted herd, which he had bought largely to oblige his uncle, Davis was forced to eat a good deal of meat which was not exactly of his choice.[8]

[7]"Indenture in Five Parts Between James McKee, J. A. Anthon, Charles Brewer, E. & H. Grimes & Davis," July 24, 1848, UCLA, is an agreement organizing the short-lived Oahu and California Mining Co. which Davis managed with the Grimeses during the Gold Rush. E. Grimes to Davis, June 8, 1848, SL, and H. Grimes to Davis, June 8, 1848, SL, contain details regarding the settlement of accounts of the shipping firm which Davis had conducted with these partners.

[8]See "Deed to Davis For A Half Interest in the Flock of Goats on Yerba Buena Island," by Nathan Spear, Oct. 9, 1848 (also signed by N. Leavenworth, Alcalde of San Francisco), MS, property of Dawson's Book Shop, Los Angeles. Davis's goats gave Goat Island its name until 1931 when the state legislature changed it to Yerba Buena, and still later to Treasure Island.

In addition to business activities, civic responsibilities were thrust upon Davis for, although still only in his mid-twenties, he was considered an oldtime American resident. In 1848 as an elected school trustee he helped establish the first American public school in San Francisco. On another occasion his cousin, Bill Howard, wrote to him: "You have been unanimously chosen by the committee of arrangements for the celebration of the fourth of July, to collect the assessments and pay demands appertaining to said celebration." Davis was also appointed treasurer, with Judge Peter H. Burnett, later the governor of California, to collect funds for the building of San Francisco's first American Catholic church.[9]

In 1849 Davis took great pride in his election to San Francisco's town council, a position he used to advantage. As a councilman, he voted to authorize the purchase of his leaky *Euphemia* as a city prison brig. Furthermore he sent aboard that tired old vessel such needed equipment as balls and chains and a barrel of handcuffs—all purchased from his store. Various persons finally attacked him and other councilmen who did business with the new city of San Francisco. There was, for example, adverse comment when he and William A. Leidesdorff sold the city fathers thousands of feet of lumber for sidewalk construction. Critics of the city council also inferred that Davis and his colleagues, as civic officials, sold themselves many valuable waterfront sites. Nevertheless before Davis bowed out of politics he received civic recognition when a street was named after him. Cousin Howard too had such a thoroughfare named in his honor.

Aside from Davis's brief membership in San Francisco's first town council, he showed only a passing interest in politics. While personable and well-liked, he seemed to possess no special

[9]Frank Soulé et al., *The Annals of San Francisco; containing a summary of the history of . . . California . . .* (New York, 1855), p. 191; Davis to J. C. Pelton, June 8, 1857, UCLA; John Cotter Pelton, *Life's Sunbeams and Shadows; poems and prose . . .* (San Francisco, 1893), pp. 219, 260, and ed. *Origin of the Free Public Schools of San Francisco; embracing the Report of the committee appointed by the Board of education of the city and county of San Francisco* (San Francisco, 1865), p. 52; *California Star*, Feb. 21, 26, May 20, 1848; Bancroft, *History*, V, 656-57; Subscription Paper, Dec. 25, 1848, Huntington MS. HM 255 (1 & 2).

political talents and demonstrated his best abilities in business. Although occasionally associated with such prominent politicians as Peter Burnett, George Hyde, and W. M. Gwin, Davis never sought to follow them into state or national politics. He once even declined a chance to represent California's Whigs at their first state convention.

Although not a politician, Davis was aroused by an important matter to which some politicians paid no attention. He was deeply concerned over the lawlessness encouraged by the Gold Rush and helped to organize American California's earliest civilian military unit, then called the "First California Guard." Upset by acts of violence that had occurred at a tent village accommodating homeless persons on his property, Davis joined a group of vigilantes organized to rout ruffians known as "the Hounds," who attacked foreign gold seekers.

The plight of many of the indigent persons bound for the mines was pitiful. For them sleeping on Davis's town lots was actually a most welcome relief. Although he charged relatively little for this, Davis and others still received substantial fees by renting tents. Good rooms rented for as much as $1,000 a month in the San Francisco of that day. Sleeping in a bunk or cot, without springs or mattress, oftentimes cost $15 a night. Up to $10 was asked for eight hours of "sleep" on tables, benches, or on other furniture. One "hospitable" San Franciscan earned $50 a night by renting half a dozen rocking chairs. Even as rude a bed rest as a redwood plank on a sawhorse brought $3 a night. A lament written by a gold seeker during the period tells the story best of all:

As for habitations nobody has anything more than a place to lie down at night under cover & thousands have not even that. A room with a bed could not be had anywhere in the city for less than $150.00 per month. One can get chances in what are called lodging houses to lie down on the floor, or perhaps stowed away in a berth with fifty others in the same room for $1 per night. Large numbers, however, unable to pay for such luxuries live in tents on the neighboring hills, sleeping upon the damp ground & many sleep under boxes, barrels & piles of lumber about the city.[10]

[10]R. R. Taylor, *Seeing the Elephant, Letters of R. R. Taylor Forty-Niner*, ed. John Walton Caughey (Los Angeles, 1951), p. 79.

Despite all the many activities in which Davis had been engaged—Gold Rush trading, membership on the city council, and vigilante responsibilities—his main concern was still the new partnership with Carter. Though enervated by the jungle climate of Panama, Carter faithfully reported various gold transactions he had arranged along the way, wrote introductions to Davis for westbound travelers, and demonstrated some of the versatility of a modern traveling salesman. At Kingston, Jamaica, he joined a group of merchants in chartering a schooner for New York, but before reaching the Atlantic coast he became desperately ill. Carter, unaware that he carried within him the germs of fast-approaching death, refused to complain of his illness.

With Carter on his way east and with their eastern trading connections inoperative, Davis found himself temporarily unable to fill orders from peddlers at the mines or from retailers in the interior. Typical of the lesser merchants who hounded Davis for goods was Robert Semple at newly founded Benicia. Semple, in writing to his partner Larkin on one occasion, was not complimentary toward his principal supplier: "Kanaka Davis, slow as he is, would leap at the opportunity" to join him, he boasted. Actually Semple could not have been more mistaken, for Davis had much larger fish to fry.

In order to obtain goods, Davis joined various San Francisco merchants in sending ships to Mazatlán in Mexico, about the only nearby West Coast port left where one might still buy eastern supplies at a decent price.[11] Davis was also involved in several of the sheep, cattle, and mule drives from Mexico which the Gold Rush touched off. With other traders he sent muleteers to Mexico to buy draft animals, in great demand at the California placers. Davis made a large profit on these speculations, although during one mule drive from Durango, almost 500 animals were confiscated by the Mexican authorities before they could cross the border.[12]

[11]Eulogio de Célis furnished $15,000 of the total $45,000 capital; Howard, Davis, Grimes, and Alphaeus Thompson invested $10,000 each.

[12]John Parrott to Davis, May 7, Aug. 26, 1849, SL. Another enterprise Davis was interested in was the furnishing of "spars" (poles) and other supplies for the telegraph.

In addition to seeking supplies in the south, Davis also sent north for them. In 1848 he joined Hensley, Reading & Company, a Sacramento firm, in a voyage to Portland, Oregon, to obtain flour, butter, and cheese for hunger-pinched San Francisco. On this journey Davis's chartered ship was frozen fast on the Columbia River. While it was "walled in by ice," other ships reached the Golden Gate loaded with Chilean flour and when Davis's cargo of cheese, butter, and flour finally arrived in the spring of 1849, it proved to be much less desirable.

All his Gold Rush ventures had not yet extinguished the lure which a voyage to China still held for Davis. One evening after dinner he confided to his house guest, José Antonio Aguirre, that he could no longer resist the temptation. Both Aguirre, who had earlier traded between Mexico and China, and Davis had considerable gold dust lying idle, and they agreed to join in chartering a ship for the Orient. Each put up $20,000, two other firms furnishing the remaining $80,000 necessary, and in June 1849, their chartered vessel, the *Rhone*, left for Canton. In her supercargo's pocket were instructions to purchase specific China goods to which the only exception was an order to buy certain engraved silver tableware from Canton and handmade furniture from Hawaii for Davis's wife.[13] After promising to bring back a cargo "such as never has yet been seen in California," the rascal returned instead with a mixed Oriental and European shipment. Though the Chinese half of the cargo netted over 100 per cent profit, Davis was forced to auction the rest on a San Francisco market which was becoming glutted. He was furious with his supercargo for not following that old adage of the sea: "Obey orders or break owners."[14]

Davis participated in several other trading ventures with Aguirre. By late 1849 both men, anxious to put to work almost $200,000 in gold dust which had accumulated in Davis's safe, chartered the bark *Rochelle* for a voyage to Chile to obtain flour. As her master they signed on old Captain Paty who, to his

[13]McKee, Anthon & Co. to Davis & Carter, Apr. 16, 1849, SL; Thomas Andrew to Davis, Jan. 18, 1848, Whitcomb Papers, printed in *Calif. Hist. Soc. Quarterly*, XXVIII (1949), 198.

[14]*75 Years*, pp. 232-49, 318-19; Davis & Carter to Wetmore & Co., Canton, China, Dec. 29, 1848 and Finley to Davis & Carter, Dec. 30, 1848, SL.

great embarrassment, experienced his first grounding in a long career at sea. The *Rochelle*, like the *Euphemia* before her, struck a rocky point on her way to Monterey from San Francisco. Fortunately Davis had recently bought the seventy-five-foot *Hortensia*, which he was also readying for a voyage to Valparaiso in search of agricultural staples, and he swiftly sailed south on her. After loading the *Rochelle's* cargo aboard Davis was about to leave for Chile when he learned that an influx of flour at San Francisco had caused a drop in prices. Had either of his two vessels departed for Chile, he would have suffered a severe financial loss. By late 1849 few items commanded the prices that characterized the early days of the Gold Rush, and business was becoming less profitable.

As the California gold bonanza drew to a close, Davis was accused of certain irregularities in his business affairs by various business associates. Once he was even threatened with legal action in connection with a voyage down the California coast when a quantity of goods disappeared from aboard his *Hortensia*. On that occasion the physician Dr. Nicholas Den of Santa Barbara charged him with lifting ten cases of champagne off his own ship.[15] On another occasion, James Hunnewell, an important Boston merchant, claimed that as his agent Davis was making short remittances for cargoes sold at San Francisco. He resented reports of hams sold at thirteen cents a pound for which other traders in California were receiving sixty. Hunnewell withheld $7,000 due Davis until he settled satisfactorily the accounts of his ships, the *New Jersey* and *Constantine*. When such tactics produced no results, the elderly Bostonian threatened suit:

I knew your parents well and I knew you in early infancy and youth and have since known you by reputation and that your means are large and I call on you to come forward and do justice. . . .[16]

Davis knew that an experienced agent like himself who could rapidly "turn around" a ship was invaluable to a distant owner

[15]Agreement between Davis, J. A. Aguirre, John Paty, and James Fitton, Oct. 5, 1849, UCLA; "Register of the San Francisco Customs House" (1850), BL.
[16]Hunnewell to Davis, Apr. 13, May 9, June 11, Nov. 25, 1850, SL.

like Hunnewell and he may have considered himself underpaid. While transient merchants dumped their merchandise into leaking dinghies or left their supplies under cover of canvas on open beaches, goods consigned to Davis were stored in cleaner, drier surroundings and pilferage was consequently reduced. From his store he skillfully sold goods for easterners; in addition, he offered them accurate intelligence about Pacific market conditions, upon which they based the movements of their ships.

If Carter, who originally established most of these eastern contacts, had been able to rejoin Davis, the pair might have become the dominant figures in the California trade of this period. Carter, however, lapsed into the final stages of his illness upon reaching Boston. While his partner lay on his deathbed Davis cheerfully wrote him about accumulating capital for even larger voyages to China and Peru, two markets in which Davis, by virtue of his increased experience, now felt qualified to trade. Not knowing that his last letter would remain unread he assured Carter, "we have made considerable, owe no one, and our business is very safe and snug."[17]

The death of Carter climaxed a series of personal misfortunes that had occurred in rapid succession. And these were far more important to him than the curtailment of future business plans. The first of his and María's many offspring suddenly died in 1849. Also his aunt, Jane Spear, who in his early youth had shown him almost maternal affection, died that year. A letter to Davis written within the crude confines of his uncle Nathan's education, in the rustic loneliness of an inland adobe, is so powerful in a husband's sense of loss and the appeal of a young son to a dead mother that it merits quotation:

Your aunt Jane is no more. . . . When I returned home she appeared to be a little unwell, but it passed off in a little time & she seemed to be well and contented. So for a day or two when she took a severe cold I was fearfull she would miscarry as she had been four months enceinte. On the morning of the 2d my fears were realized. She took another cold which denied her of speech and hearing, a high fever settled & she died on the 6th.

[17]Davis to Carter, Apr. 9, 1849, SL. In a letter of Feb. 7, 1849, Davis reported to Carter the sale of cargoes at enormous profits, having recently handled one bought at Valparaiso for $60,000 and sold at San Francisco for $350,000.

Grate God William, can you imagine my feelings. Poor little William, he came to the bed side a few moments before his mother died & said kiss ma, ma, O God I can write no more. I am blind.[18]

Spear himself lived only a year longer. With his death, Davis lost his only relation in California. The two men who had brought him his greatest success and with whom he felt most comfortable were now gone. Carter's was a short friendship, but the relationship with Spear was very close and extended back to boyhood days. Without the company of these two men and with the Gold Rush coming to an end, Davis felt that he faced an uncertain future.

There were, of course, his Hawaiian relatives and Davis kept up his contacts with them. He tried to tell María Jesús about the family there but was unable successfully to explain how differently his far-off relations lived. Her opinion of them was not improved by their constant appeals for money. Nor was William pleased, as he once might have been, by their frequent intimations that he was becoming a Gold Rush millionaire. He looked for understanding in his time of stress and instead was asked for help. He sent them cool replies. Yet he seemed unable to forget the Hawaii of his youth in spite of the unhappiness caused him by several years of legal disputes over various family lands with the very relatives who asked for his aid. William was also forced to worry about the family's cattle herds—the Davis family still owned about 1,000 head despite his mother's large sales before her death. It was difficult to hold the runaway mavericks to small pastures and Robert often called on William to help pay fines levied against the trespassing cattle. Eventually these tough and bony beasts were sold for about five cents a pound. Income from a cooper shop and several other Honolulu buildings diminished so steadily that William turned most of them over to his brother and their half-sister, Elizabeth.[19]

[18]Spear to Davis, Nov. 10, 1848, UCLA; San Francisco *Alta California*, Nov. 8, 1849; Letter and Transcript of William N. Spear, July 28, 1877, Bancroft Library MSS.

[19]Semple to Larkin, July 27, 1848, LP; Semple to Davis, July 23, 1847, Bancroft Library MSS; Reynolds to Davis, Mar. 1, Sept. 1, 1848, SL. Problems involved in raising cattle in Hawaii are discussed in Andrew F. Rolle, "Rancho Tropical," *Southwestern Historical Quarterly*, XLIX (1945), 307-308.

Family troubles in Hawaii and the more serious personal sorrows were becoming more bearable now that Davis had the companionship of his wife. With her help he emerged from the gold bonanza with a considerable fortune made by mastering the illusive techniques of trading. John Walton Caughey has termed the financially wisest Gold Rush participants those who, like Davis, turned not to the diminishing rewards of the placers but to "hauling or farming, or dish washing, where the compensation was not only surer but higher." Supplying the California mines had been one of these less glamorous but highly lucrative pursuits. The flush years of the Gold Rush, though they had quickly enriched Davis, had also sidetracked his normal storekeeping career. Those years had provided too many speculative distractions.

A FTER THE GOLD RUSH a wave of migration continued to engulf the Far West, and soon Davis became involved in building cities, roads, and other needed facilities for California's countless newcomers. Providing an adequate water transport system to accommodate the many rootless persons returning from the mines now interested him especially. Davis knew that he could profit handsomely from the many people who wanted transportation from the interior to the coast. But first he had to find a substitute vessel for the *Euphemia*, moored on San Francisco's waterfront where she had already become a landmark as the community's prison brig.[1]

Transportation problems were not new to Davis. During the Gold Rush he had taken many gold-crazed travelers up the river on the small launches he used to deliver supplies to Sacramento. Now he and others determined to expand such services. They realized this commerce was only a prelude to a permanent passenger service that would keep many vessels busy churning the waters of California's major river.

While trying to capitalize on the opportunity to enter this river traffic Davis, largely through circumstances beyond his control, lost his best chance to make a large fortune. Early in 1849 he joined John Parrott, a speculator of great promise, and William A. Richardson, a friend of long standing, in plans to

[1]A picture of the *Euphemia* appears opposite p. 606 in Eldredge, *Beginnings of San Francisco* and in 75 *Years*, p. 261. A stylized drawing and description of the ship is in Miriam Allen DeFord, "When San Quentin was a Ship," *Westways*, XLIV (1952), 16.

build a shallow-draft steam vessel. With them Davis signed an agreement to subscribe a capital outlay of $45,000. Unfortunately when Parrott went to the eastern shipyards to arrange for construction of a ship, he encountered unexpected competition from other western speculators who also planned to build such sternwheelers. Without telling Davis he abandoned the shipping enterprise and sent him thirty-one prefabricated iron houses to sell. Meanwhile, unaware of the change of plans, Davis not only bought river-front property at Sacramento on which to build a depot, but also sold some of his best San Francisco holdings, later worth several large fortunes. Parrott apologetically sent Mrs. Davis a Concord carriage, one of San Francisco's first. But Davis never forgave him for abandoning their steamship project. He could only record his disappointment prosaically by stating, "The business would have produced for us hundreds of thousands if not a million or more dollars."[2]

Davis was not exaggerating the earnings which their company might have gained. For once an enterprising promoter, Lafayette Maynard, convinced various partners that deep-draft ocean-going steamers could navigate the Sacramento, Maynard and his eastern associates began a steamship business that made a tremendous profit. When Davis joined a group of speculators who tried to buy Maynard's sidewheeler, the *Senator*, their offer of $250,000 in gold was answered only by the smiles of Maynard's partners. The vessel was soon to earn her owners $50,000 a week. Loading her decks "black with living humanity," they charged $50 a person for the trip from Sacramento to San Francisco and Maynard boasted to a correspondent:

The Senator will make in the next 12 months $1,000,000, nor let this startle you for I assure you that in the three trips that she has made she has averaged that sum.[3]

[2]Parrott to Davis, June 23, 1849, SL, and Aug. 1, 1850, UCLA; Bancroft, *History*, IV, 768, describes Parrott as known "for never taking any risks, his caution and conservatism being in marked contrast with the prevalent spirit of the times."

[3]"Two Letters of Lafayette Maynard and an Excerpt From William Heath Davis Relative to the Steamer 'Senator,'" *Calif. Hist. Soc. Quarterly*, XVI (1937), 73; John Haskell Kemble, "The 'Senator,' the Biography of a Pioneer Steamship," *ibid.*, 61-70.

After failing to buy the *Senator* or to build his own ship, Davis became involved in founding a short-lived shipping firm called the California Steam Packet Company to provide service between San Francisco and Panama. Its president was his old friend Larkin, whose motive in forming the new organization was the restoration of ocean-going service to Benicia—after the Gold Rush Benicia had been dropped as a port of call by the Pacific Mail Steamship Company. Although Davis raised $600,000 in an abortive attempt to challenge that organization's entrenched position, he resigned as treasurer when the directors levied each stockholder $10,000 for operating expenses.

In a period when an iron will was of indispensable benefit to those emerging western capitalists whose only goal was success, Davis vacillated in making crucial decisions. He frequently would begin an operation and then drop it after what sometimes was the slightest provocation. This element of indecision in his character contributed to his loss of leadership in various fields. Such was the case in his wharf-building activities as well as in his abortive attempts to enter the steamship business.[4] Nevertheless, for a time, he continued to make a good deal of money.

A rapid inflation of San Francisco property values temporarily made Davis a wealthy man. Edwin Bryant's early book, *What I Saw In California*, described him as among the three principal merchants who owned the most property at a time when small buildings were rented at over $4,000 a month. In the San Francisco of that day the two-story Parker House, which cost only $30,000 to build, rented for $120,000 a year. The El Dorado gambling saloon, a canvas tent twenty-five by fifteen feet square, brought $40,000 a year to its owners. Davis sold small lots for $8,000 which the city but a few years before consigned to him for about $15.

Encouraged by this acceleration of his good fortune Davis began, in September 1849, to construct San Francisco's first brick building of more than one story. This four-story edifice,

---

[4]Davis to Larkin, Albert Priest, and J. P. Thompson, Apr. 30, 1850, "Davis Letterbook," SL; Davis to California Steam Packet Co., June 18, 1850, and to W. H. Tiffany, June 18, 1850, SL.

most of whose building materials came from Boston, was on the corner of Montgomery and California streets. While still under construction it attracted the attention of a group (including Commodore Thomas Ap Catesby Jones, commander of the United States Pacific Squadron) that hoped to relocate San Francisco near the Carquinez Straits. On their behalf Jones made a proposal to Davis to rebuild the structure at Benicia. The commodore ostensibly offered to transport the building materials there at no cost to Davis. Though Jones, like Larkin and Semple, had an interest in Benicia, it was unusual for a senior naval officer on active duty to make such overtures. Davis later insisted that he was under considerable pressure "to give up the city that I had assisted to build from its infancy, and to establish my large business at Benicia."[5]

But Davis remained in San Francisco. When he finally completed his brick building he leased it to the federal government as a customs house for the then reasonable rental of $36,000 a year. He was about to raise its rent to $100,000 when the structure was suddenly lost to him.[6]

Fire was the enemy that consumed his most important investment. With neither bells to sound alarms nor pump engines to fight the flames, six great fires swept over San Francisco in a period of eighteen months. In 1851 the last of these proved to be the most disastrous. The only protection available against the conflagration was a bucket brigade that plastered the walls of buildings with water and liquid mud from street bogs. But this scarcely quelled the enemy. Fire destroyed much of the city and among the ashes lay the ruins of the new customs house. The building was almost totally demolished—along with its cache of bonded goods—from basement to roof. Davis managed to salvage only $3,000, a month's rent. Fortunately a warehouse which he owned was saved. These and other properties had been grossing an income of over $10,000 a month—a considerable

[5] T. A. Barry & B. A. Patten, *Men and Memories of San Francisco, in the "Spring of '50"* (San Francisco, 1873), p. 241; *75 Years*, pp. 316-17; Davis to J. Collier, Dec. 22, 1849, "Davis Letterbook," SL.

[6] Agreement between Jotham Rogers and Davis, Nov. 5, 1849, UCLA; *75 Years*, pp. 316-17.

sum during the mid-nineteenth century. Davis estimated that he lost about three-quarters of a million dollars in the smoke that hovered over the Golden Gate.[7]

It would have taken more than the six emergency hogsheads full of water atop his customs house to put out the fire of 1851. Once the exterior wooden staircase was consumed, flames enveloped the building and there was no way to move from one floor to another. A good friend, Bernard Peyton, who was in the building, was badly burned and escaped only by wrapping himself in a blanket. A still older acquaintance, Captain George Vincent, was burned alive.

Although the fire was a major disaster for Davis,[8] there were still other reasons why his financial operations began to falter. Had he continued to pay serious attention to the merchandising and trading that had already made him a "paper-fortune" of several million dollars, he might have kept this wealth. But he could not seem to realize his limitations nor recognize his real forte. While he was suited to the pastoral life that had existed in California before the conquest he did not seem fully able to cope with the new society. It is not unlikely that he knew this but he sometimes fought against it. Because he refused to accept the role of a small businessman and trader, much of the remainder of his life was one of frustration. He continued, often indecisively, to entertain grandiose schemes and to seek new speculations. But none of these led him to return to his northern trading business where he had gained his position and wealth.

[7] *75 Years*, pp. 316-17; Bancroft, *History*, VI, 263; Soulé, *Annals*, pp. 334-38.

[8] Before the fatal fire Thomas Butler King, San Francisco's port collector, had insisted on costly alterations to the customs house. Faced with the prospect of King's election to the Senate, and wishing to protect the future rental of his building, Davis had spent large sums on the structure.

# CHAPTER VIII

## FOUNDING AMERICAN SAN DIEGO*

ABOUT A YEAR before the San Francisco fire of 1851 a still affluent Davis had become interested in an ambitious plan to build a new city outside the old pueblo of San Diego. Over the years Davis had come to know San Diego intimately. He had first sailed into its harbor at the age of nine and had returned many times thereafter. From the San Diego branch of his wife's family he learned much about the old town whose small population was huddled, in Spanish colonial tradition, near its adobe presidio. The most progressive residents deplored the distance of their town from the water's edge, and from personal experience Davis knew the handicap of transporting cargoes from the beach to the pueblo in wagons.

That the city's original site was unfavorable to its growth was reiterated to Davis by Andrew Belcher Gray, chief surveyor for the United States Boundary Commission which visited San Diego in 1849. After the commission had camped on a sandy waterfront shelf during numerous balmy June nights, Gray visualized for Davis the building of a long overdue American San Diego. He thought that the very spot where the commission had bivouacked, Punto de los Muertos, was a more logical and accessible location for a seaport than where the Spaniards had first built their city in 1769.

Davis first heard Gray's ideas when, following a physician's advice, he went south for a rest. He agreed that a town located

*A different version of this chapter was published as "William Heath Davis and the Founding of American San Diego," *Calif. Hist. Soc. Quarterly*, XXXI (1952), 33-48 and reprinted as a booklet by the San Diego Title Insurance Co. (1952).

at the water's edge would prosper and soon the two men were making plans for such a community. In the tradition of generations of frontier town founders Davis took an unpremeditated plunge into a new world of financial uncertainty, a leap from which he never recovered his equilibrium.

To free himself for the building of New Town Davis kept aloof from further shipping activities at San Francisco. His plans to enter the steamship business were in the past and he even wrote the late Carter's friends to place their western business in other hands. Fortunately Davis never entirely succeeded in closing down his northern interests while engaged in the San Diego venture.[1]

Twenty-eight years old and at the pinnacle of his financial success, Davis now launched the construction of an American San Diego. About to undertake an experiment which ultimately inspired a modern city, he had obviously reached another turning point in his career. He was, furthermore, able to induce others to view the New Town project through his rose-colored glasses. Widely respected, serious but friendly, he attracted many others to the project. As the main investor, Davis on March 16, 1850, signed a partnership agreement with Andrew Gray, José Antonio Aguirre, Miguel de Pedrorena, and William C. Ferrell for the development of the new town site. They obtained a land grant of about 160 acres from the local alcalde for a few thousand dollars to which Davis, "being flush, and having a large income," added additional land bought from Miguel de Pedrorena.[2]

At the outset prospects for New Town seemed bright. California had recently been admitted to the Union and San Diego was one of its most attractive counties. The termination of the Gold Rush brought thousands of persons south to a warmer climate; some thought New Town might even depopulate La Playa and Old Town, the two settlements that comprised the San Diego of that day. These communities, already rivals over the site of

<hr>

[1]Davis to Hunnewell, Dec. 31, 1849, Apr. 19, 1850, "Davis Letterbook," SL.

[2]"William C. Ferrell—Kangaroo Mice," Huntington MS. DA 2(171); *60 Years*, p. 367. Original deed for beach lots purchased from Pedrorena, Feb. 26, 1850, in Pedrorena Folder, Historical Miscellanea, San Diego Hist. Soc.; *History of San Diego County With Illustrations* (San Francisco, 1883), p. 88.

the future San Diego, eyed Davis's plans with suspicion. His operations became especially suspect after he persuaded the military to build an Army depot at New Town by offering Lieutenant Thomas D. Johns, quartermaster and commissary of a cargo of government-owned lumber, a share in the new community.[3]

Davis, the ambitious town planner, was a picture of activity as he supervised the many aspects of building the new city. After a scientist, Dr. John L. Le Conte, surveyed his site, Davis built a $60,000 wharf for which he furnished and transported from San Francisco the spruce, yellow pine planks, men and machinery needed for its construction.[4] It was Davis who provided the mule teams for freighting these supplies from shipside to the building sites; it was Davis who raised most of the money for the thousands of bricks brought around the Horn on ships like the *Cybele*; and it was Davis who hauled from Sausalito and the Albion River on his own *Hortensia* the many redwood piles, girders, and thousands of feet of lumber necessary to construct houses, stores, and his own residence—San Diego's first frame house—still standing over 100 years later.[5]

New Town's promoters wisely gave a tract of land to the government on which to build the San Diego Barracks and from 1852 to 1920 several hundred men were usually stationed there. From this army supply depot merchandise unloaded at Davis's wharf was wagon-freighted as far north as Fort Tejon and as far east as Yuma. Eventually the scarcity of water forced the installation of a cistern at the post to catch rain. His new saloon, Pan-

[3]William E. Smythe, *History of San Diego, 1542-1907; an account of the rise and progress of the pioneer settlement on the Pacific coast of the United States* (San Diego, 1908), I, 316-18; Walter Gifford Smith, *The Story of San Diego* (San Diego, 1892), pp. 96-101.

[4]Johns to Davis, June 24, 1850 and C. H. Hill to Davis, Aug. 29, 1850, MS Letters, San Diego Pioneers, 1850-1855, Pasadena Public Library, Pasadena, Calif. Hereafter cited as PPL. *An Illustrated History of Southern California* (Chicago, 1890), p. 28; San Diego *Herald*, July 31, 1851; *Senate Report No. 207*, 46th Cong., 2d sess. (Washington, 1880), pp. 1-2.

[5]*60 Years*, pp. 533-34. The *Cybele's* cargo included 300,000 bricks. Davis's house, also shipped on the *Cybele*, was originally located on State Street between G and H; W. A. Richardson to Davis, Jan. 25, 1851, "Davis Letterbook," Calif. Hist. Soc., San Francisco.

toja House, advertised as a "resort for gentlemen," also helped relieve San Diego's water shortage.

John Russell Bartlett, the United States Boundary Commissioner then out west, was not impressed with New Town:

A large and fine wharf was built here at great expense; but there is no business to bring vessels here, except an occasional one with government stores. There is no water nearer than the San Diego River, three miles distant. . . . wood has to be brought some eight or ten miles; nor is there any arable land within four miles. Without wood, water, or arable land this place can never rise to importance. . . .[6]

Despite Bartlett's pessimism, a shaky city mushroomed around a plaza called Pantoja Park. The San Diego Hotel soon advertised rooms for rent and various merchants, including Davis, earnestly began businesses. Gray built "the Hermitage" as his residence, while the later Civil War generals Nathaniel Lyon and J. Bankhead Magruder, still junior officers, established homes near their post at New Town.

Davis hoped that his city would attract a newspaper and his wish was fulfilled by the arrival of a journalist, John Judson Ames. He came from New Orleans across Panama, and lugged along a hand press which he almost lost in the waters of the Chagres River. On it Ames printed the first copy of his San Diego *Herald*, only twelve days after the Los Angeles *Star*, southern California's earliest newspaper, first appeared. Later the *Herald* attracted national attention under that celebrated guest editor and satirical humorist Lt. George P. Derby, alias John Phoenix. Although the newspaper frequently changed hands, Davis loyally continued to back each incumbent publisher.

The *Herald* soon announced the establishment at New Town of commission merchants, notaries, and storekeepers. The town's founders were, of course, most prominent in its daily life. Thomas Johns resigned his army commission to conduct a coal-refueling business which supplied the occasional steamers that called at their new wharf. Pedrorena contemplated awarding one city lot to the masters of ships who encouraged others to dock there.

[6]*Personal Narrative of Explorations and incidents in Texas, New Mexico, California, Sonora, and Chihuahua* . . . (New York, 1854), II, 97.

Unfortunately Gray, who had returned east to render the report of his boundary commission, failed to arrange for Aspinwall steamers to stop at New Town. But he did succeed in getting other companies to use Davis's wharf. When the 1500-ton Vanderbilt vessel *Pacific* was due there, he urged Davis to give its captain "a blow out when he arrives."[7]

Davis, who was appointed San Diego agent for the Vanderbilt ships, hoped to establish a local coaling station and a telegraph connection from San Diego to San Francisco. His capital, however, became tighter as time passed for he found few trading opportunities at his San Diego store. Though Davis now devoted little time to his San Francisco operations, he traveled north to draw upon those investments everytime he was pinched for money. While away, he entrusted his San Diego saloon, billiard rooms, and store to various assistants.

Whenever Davis was in the north, his wife had only a Negro cook, Francisco, and their infant daughter, Anita, to keep her company. María was with child again by 1850 and grew tired of her husband's absences. For María the founding of American San Diego had meant forsaking their fine San Francisco home and moving far from her beloved family at San Leandro. Her husband shipped all their furniture south and frequently gave her such presents as sets of English bone china, but this did not make up for her lonesomeness, especially when Davis stayed away for weeks. When, partly to please her, Davis resigned from those remaining northern financial interests which kept him away from their San Diego home, he thereby cut his ties with the expanding maritime prosperity of San Francisco.

Once his New Town was almost built Davis, thinking himself free of routine business chores in the south as well as in the north, turned more of his attention toward pleasure. He indulged in those entertainments which a man of his means could afford. Visits to the north often led him elsewhere than to his place of business. He frequented the very best resorts and was particularly fond of warm springs as places to relax. Davis seldom squandered money, but he lived a full life while he could afford it.

[7]Gray to Davis, Apr. 27, 1851, UCLA.

After selling his San Francisco home he usually stayed in hotels while visiting the city. That oasis of the West had already begun to achieve a cosmopolitan atmosphere and a reputation for excellent French and Italian cuisine.[8] And these qualities Davis much enjoyed.

As New Town developed so did its problems. The San Diego *Herald*'s pages suggest that the city "was infested with rowdies, adventurers, and drifters" who on one occasion "turned to and stoned a poor Indian" to death; the newspaper lamented the fact that such events would "probably be repeated." The jail threw doubt upon its contractor's honesty. A brief downpour of rain showed that the building had been erected with cementless mortar. A prisoner, later found celebrating at a local bar, admitted that he had dug his way out of this jail with a penknife. Davis underestimated the weakness of the city and overestimated its strength. He did not seem to understand what he had to do to insure the success of his project.

Frequently his attention was diverted to relatively unimportant matters. Like other successful men of that era, he took pride in owning several fine carriages and teams of horses. He derived particular satisfaction from driving a pair of fast stallions down the country roads that had already begun to supplant California's cowpaths. On such rides when his wanderlust got the best of him Davis sometimes traveled into the interior, as had been his custom when he visited rancheros as a supercargo. His absences from San Diego for weeks at a time proved ill-advised and costly.

In 1851 Davis, in a lighthearted mood, accompanied the nephews of former Governor Argüello on a gold hunt into Lower California. Organized in part to attract settlers to nearby New Town, the party journeyed through uninviting country to hunt for a mine whose location was known only to a few Indians. To no avail Davis promised these natives whole bales of calicoes, blankets, and tobacco, in order to gain information about the whereabouts of this gold, but he returned empty-handed. The

[8]See Pauline Jacobson, *City of the Golden 'Fifties* (Berkeley, 1941) and Julia Altrocchi, *The Spectacular San Franciscans* (New York, 1949). San Francisco, although not yet the scene of its later elegance, was already clearly different from the place in which Davis had founded his early fortune.

trip, which drew no settlers to New Town as predicted, was but another instance wherein his money was drained away.

Illustrative of the altered judgment Davis had in business matters was the way in which he almost became involved in other chimerical enterprises. The discovery of some coal specimens of dubious origin in a shaft outside New Town nearly convinced him that he should organize a coal company. Only a sobering geological report by Professor Le Conte stopped him from embarking upon this undertaking.[9]

Plunging deeper into his commitments at San Diego, Davis was frequently assured by Gray that he would have the satisfaction of being the founder of a great metropolis. "Ten years— and you will still be young—and will be surrounded by a delightful population," Gray wrote. He also advised Davis to build more houses to accommodate large crowds of people who would soon be descending on their new city:

Davis, attach to your wharf—where it passes over the sand spit—a bathing house for ladies and gentlemen. . . . this would be a great attraction and profitable also.[10]

In effect, Gray had become Davis's eastern agent and he joined the many people who appeared in Washington on behalf of town developers from all over the country. They went to the national capital to argue with congressmen and other federal officials about such matters as land titles, taxation, and internal improvements. Gray tried interminably to convince the Post Office Department to open a branch at New Town. Davis also engaged several agents to talk personally with the Secretary of the Treasury about moving La Playa's customs house to New Town, a

[9]Davis to Le Conte, July 31, 1850, SL; Professor Le Conte was mapping the faunal areas of the West. On Le Conte see Samuel H. Scudder, "John Lawrence Le Conte," in National Academy of Sciences, *Biographical Memoirs* (Washington, 1886), II, 263-93, and *Dictionary of American Biography* (New York, 1933), XI, 89-90.

[10]Gray to Davis, Mar. 8, July 31, 1851, UCLA and SL. Other friends who also waxed eloquent and invested heavily there included Davis's brother, Robert, the Mormon merchant Sam Brannan, Captain George Vincent, the artist Edward Vischer, the San Francisco banker Bernard Peyton, and Captain Paty. See Vincent to Davis, May 22, 1850, SL; Davis to Vischer, June 17, 1850, and Vischer to Davis, Mar. 1, July 1, 31, Aug. 31, 1850, SL.

suggestion that never bore fruit and that only irritated the community's city fathers.[11]

By late 1851 Davis found that his sources of wealth were drying up and he gave various eastern agents confidential instructions to sell out his New Town holdings if a good price could be obtained from people interested in building a railroad to the West. But such an offer was never made and in order to get capital for New Town, he liquidated property in northern California which he should have retained.

New Town simply did not attract the population Davis and his partners expected. As his investments soured, almost everything seemed to be failing. To add to his troubles, the uneconomical and worm-eaten *Hortensia* lay rotting in the waters of San Diego Bay. Forced by the lack of transportation to buy the brig *Ryan* for $10,600 Davis saw only debts piling up:

All the funds that I have drawn from the store and other sources have been eaten up in the expenses of the town, coal company, vessels, etc.—without me God only knows what they would do here—it has taken an enormous sum to meet all their demands. We meet with much opposition from the inhabitants of the old town and beach—they make every effort in the world to crush us. . . . I am on my back and unwell.[12]

In an attempt to salvage his northern holdings, Davis went to San Francisco where he learned how little business he had left. With the Gold Rush several years in the past money had become scarce. Huddled in his store—the only source of revenue left him—he tended to shun the debacle further south, no matter how loud María's complaints. A few days at the Golden Gate made him realize that his northern business had been badly managed. His store was glutted with thousands of high-priced Mexican "segars" which were now rancid and unsalable. To meet his losses, the merchant sold San Francisco property for one-tenth its real value to Hall McAllister and William T. Cole-

[11]J. G. Brown to Thomas Corwin (Secretary of the Treasury), Feb. 10, 1852 and Corwin to W. C. Fennellsey, Feb. 20, 1852, SL.

[12]Davis to C. W. Lawton, June 18, July 16, 1850, SL; "Cargo Book of the Barque *Hortensia*, 1849-1850," UCLA.

man, harbingers of a new type in San Francisco. Davis was participating in a process by which a new group of financial giants, who later built their brownstone mansions on Nob Hill, supplanted his circle of pre-pioneer settlers.

Those funds which were not poured down the interminable economic drain at San Diego were consumed by taxes up north. His San Francisco tax assessments soared, as the citizens voted for expensive boardwalks to replace local mud bogs and for other civic improvements.

In addition to problems in San Francisco, a succession of troubles in San Diego continued to plague Davis. Even Pantoja House, his billiard room and saloon, the only investment in the south which had provided him with income, was now failing due to a combination of dishonesty, poor management, and a lack of business. Davis complained to a friend, "The man I had put in charge has absconded and walked off with about $2,000 of my money, so you see, that one misfortune follows another." His three San Diego agents once compared notes and reported selling "in one day between us the sum of two dollars and twelve cents!" One of them lamented that he was not selling enough to pay for his billiard losses, and "I lose very few games," he boasted.[13]

At San Diego some of the large houses Davis had built went begging at $800 and he was fortunate to sell smaller ones for $300. Attempting to recoup some of these losses, Davis shipped unused lumber and house frames to San Francisco. More remunerative was his transporting of newly built houses across San Diego Bay to Old Town where that rival community's residents had the satisfaction of seeing them sold below cost. These attempts to raise money indicated the straits into which Davis had sunk.

As New Town's business deteriorated its merchants, like its buildings, drifted over to Old Town. By 1853 the *Herald* had moved there too. Johns eventually closed down his coal business and departed for San Francisco, while traders like Ferrell left

[13]W. F. Toler to Davis, Aug. 20, Sept. 21, Nov. 5, 1851, PPL; G. F. Hooper to Davis, May 18, 1851 and John Cook to Davis, May 16, 1851, PPL; San Diego *Herald*, May 29, 1851.

for Lower California. A dwindling group of diehards—not including Davis—lingered longest in houses that had been built around Pantoja Park. His own residence, from which he and María formally departed late in 1851, was rented by a succession of agents. The remaining houses that were not torn down eventually formed the nucleus of a town whose founders bought lots from Davis for as low as sixty cents each.

Perhaps it is true that a fortune must be lost before a new one can be gained for often the followers in a venture capitalize upon the work of the innovators. The credit for the founding of American San Diego has until recently gone not to Davis but to Alonzo Erastus Horton, a speculator who followed him considerably later. Only a few have questioned that distinction. One local historian has, however, suggested that "perhaps the most fitting name for modern San Diego would have been Davis," and a land title executive, once president of the San Diego Chamber of Commerce, has called Davis the "real father" of San Diego.[14]

In an unpublished manuscript Davis himself later repudiated the idea that Horton was the founder of the city.[15] In the sixties Davis was given an opportunity to join a group which planned to fight Horton by building a new community south of San Diego. But still deficient in capital, he refused and thereby lost his last chance for prominence at San Diego. Many persons thereafter referred to New Town's short existence as "Davis' Folly." As early as September 1851, San Francisco's *Alta California* had spoken of the venture as "a most disastrous speculation, an immense amount having been sunk in the operation." Perhaps out of friendship for him, the historian Hubert Howe Bancroft hardly mentioned the fiasco in his writings.

In some respects Davis deserved more credit than he received. In recent celebrations of California's centennial years much attention was paid to her Gold Rush, to American acquisition, and to the province's evolution into statehood. Forgotten, how-

[14]Winifred Davidson, "Historical Miscellanea," San Diego Hist. Soc. MS; San Diego *Union*, Aug. 10, 1940. Almost a century earlier the *Herald* (Oct. 9, 1851) had eulogized contributions of Davis to San Diego.

[15]"Founders of the City of San Diego," Huntington MS. DA 2 (280); Smythe, *San Diego*, pp. 319-20.

ever, were the sacrifices made by the many town builders like Davis who, too early for their own benefit, tried to create order out of confusion. By attempting to provide stopovers for dusty travelers such men anticipated the growth in population that would make their communities more than a collection of rude shacks. In a remote corner of the United States his experiment, though patently unsuccessful, forms a part of the largely unwritten urban history of the American West.

When one considers the general picture of western urban development it is obvious that, in addition to his own short-comings, Davis did not succeed as a town founder for a variety of reasons. New Town's inability to attract population was only one of several handicaps that help explain the community's failure during the 1850's. A water shortage proved so serious that army units stationed there were forced to send a daily water train several miles away to the meagerly supplied San Diego River. In his search for water Davis spent a small fortune boring wells after a visiting sea captain told him: "Get water, get water and your place is made." The choice of New Town's location rested too much on its land-locked harbor and mild climate. Such essentials as building materials and foodstuffs had to be carted into the town over long distances. For years the residents were forced to depend upon mule teams described as traveling "from nowhere to nowhere." Even more important, a three-cornered fight between New Town, Old Town and La Playa helped to spell the doom of the community. The discouragement of prospective settlers by the two other communities kept New Town, even at its height, to less than 250 residents. Although a sizable enough nucleus the population gradually dwindled, and this was another reason why prospective residents shied away from the place.

Still other factors influenced the decline of American San Diego. In 1852 the city charter was repealed. The same year the local treasury was depleted by officials who were often too busy carousing to be good civic servants. Also, a nearby Indian uprising, which even received publicity in the Philadelphia *Public Ledger and Transcript* for January 2, 1852, frightened prospective settlers away from New Town. As the city and its harbor sank into a deep slumber, Davis was warned repeatedly by his accountant to "take some measures to extinguish mounting debts to avoid paying so much interest. It will make a hole in your estate." But even with loans from his brother, Davis simply could not pay his debts. All his plans seemed to be going awry.[16]

Eventually his San Diego wharf lay largely in disuse, and no one even bothered to collect a modest wharfage fee of $10 from shipmasters. An adjoining warehouse was likewise used "free of charge." In 1853 two steamer captains proposed that they be given free wharfage for agreeing to anchor their ships at New Town! That same year Davis heard from his agents that his wharf had been run into by a steamer and was seriously damaged. They reported that some thirty feet of the wharf, "the most valuable part, it being the only berth where vessels of deep draft could lay," was torn away.[17] All these heartaches made Davis wish he had never heard the name San Diego.

The story of Davis's defeat at San Diego does not end with his abandonment of the city and the movement of his family back to San Francisco in 1851. For many years thereafter he was harassed by a succession of disappointments in the south. During that long period Davis almost sold his damaged wharf to various financiers. Once a Mr. Comstock, whose poke of money was reputedly as large as the Nevada lode of the same name, offered him $10,000 for the wharf, but Davis refused to sell. During the late fifties still another bid of $25,000 was made, this time for the whole of New Town. By his refusal of such sums Davis lost the opportunity to get rid of a financial millstone at a time when the wharf's piles were described as so brittle that they were "snapping like pipe stems." He seemed to be refusing to admit a defeat already in existence despite the fact that the San Diego enterprise was draining away his savings.

During the Civil War the greatest damage to his unguarded San Diego properties occurred. His agents there decried both New Town's dilapidated appearance and the foraging of trespassing army units which had just destroyed Davis's store:

[16]Peyton to Davis, Jan. 15, 1851, UCLA.

[17]Ames & Pendleton to Davis, Sept. 27, 1853 and E. B. Pendleton to Davis, June 27, 1853, PPL; San Diego *Herald*, Mar. 19, and July 9, 1853.

. . . you are indebted to the *California Volunteers* for appropriating it to their own use for various purposes and lastly for firewood. . . . Pantoja House shared the same fate at the hands of these miserable specimens of humanity in Uncle Sam's uniform who enlisted because they were too lazy to work.[18]

By then even the outhouses had long since disappeared; poachers from Lower California also took fences, window sashes, and doors to "pack them off hundreds of miles."

His property might have been damaged less seriously if Davis had not been so far distant. During a trip south to San Diego in 1871 he managed to sell some sixty-five lots for an average of $500 each. Earlier he had sacrificed the bulk of his holdings for about a dollar a lot in order to satisfy tax liens and to placate the many squatters who had settled on the abandoned lands.

By the early seventies Davis hit upon the idea of instituting a claim against the United States Government for the Civil War demolishment of his San Diego properties. He believed that two regiments, passing from San Francisco to Arizona in the winter of 1861-1862, caused most of the damage. At Washington, where Davis faced years of expensive lobbying, he persistently urged numerous congressmen to introduce compensatory legislation to reimburse his claims for $60,000 damages. Although his appeal finally reached Congress in 1872, it was not placed on the calendar of private business until the forty-sixth Congress of 1880.[19]

Among the many friends who sent messages to Washington on his behalf were three former governors of California, several state senators, various jurists, and members of the Society of California Pioneers. Davis also reminded the government, in a mimeographed pamphlet, of his donation of some $20,000 worth of land for its use and of the failure of "Congress after Congress" to appropriate "a just and equitable amount."

His travels to collect evidence in support of his claim gave friends of Davis an opportunity to honor him at numerous

[18]G. A. Pendleton to Davis, July 13, 1867, UCLA.

[19]"House Resolution 6247," *House Report No. 1465*, 46th Cong., 2d sess. (Washington, 1880), p. 1, and "House Resolution 6860," *House Report. No. 84*, 46th Cong. 3d sess. (Washington, 1881), p. 1; printed letter, May 18, 1881, Hqs., Mil. Div. Pacific & Dept. Calif., UCLA.

San Francisco in 1847 — from the hill back.

(*From the collection of Hutton Drawings, Henry E. Huntington Library*)

receptions. At San Diego in 1880, he and his wife were swept off their feet by local hospitality. An old acquaintance cautioned: "Now my dear friend take good care of yourself and you and Mrs. Davis must not *dance too* much when at parties. *Be moderate*." These celebrations, unfortunately, hurt their pocketbook. Travel by carriage throughout the state to obtain witnesses in support of his claim was expensive. In 1881 he wrote an acquaintance from the Pico House in Los Angeles: "My limited purse is now reduced to $11—and I must hang on to that for my personal expenses in the city."[20]

When his heavy loans could not be repaid, Davis assigned most of his pending San Diego claim to an old friend for one dollar. His San Francisco friends wrote to the aging pioneer that he was "too good a man" to deserve such torture. In colorful language one of them expressed resentment of the government's indecision which made it necessary for Davis to stay so long in Washington: "If it was not for the most wonderful hope and perseverance you possess I know you would have left months since and told them all to go to that place where gold and silver will melt in their pockets. . . ."[21]

In 1882 Congress considered a resolution based upon a favorable report of his claim from the Army Quartermaster General to award Davis $20,000. Robert Todd Lincoln, Secretary of War, in transmitting the results of his investigation to the Speaker of the House recommended, instead, that Davis be paid only $3,000 with 6 per cent interest from 1862.[22]

By 1885 a still undecided Congress had printed hundreds of pages of testimony concerning the case, testimony costing thousands of dollars. Tired of wrangling over the matter, the Senate, in a dull moment, once even decided it had no authority

[20]Davis to J. B. Metcalfe, July 7, 1881, SL.

[21]Ferdinand Vassault to Davis, Oct. 9, 12, Dec. 16, 1880, SL; Mar. 5, 11, 1882, UCLA, are letters of condolence from a well-known San Francisco pioneer.

[22]In *House Report No. 1358*, 47th Cong., 1st sess. (Washington, 1882), pp. 1-2, Congress recommended various amounts of money to remunerate Davis. These ranged from a peak of $60,000 to the sum of $3,000 plus accrued interest (or $6,570) suggested in *House Exec. Doc. No. 9*, 47th Cong., 1st sess. (Washington, 1882), p. 1. The latter is a ninety-one-page accumulation of testimony concerning the Davis claim.

to remunerate and referred the case to a court of claims. For a time it looked as though Davis's years of work had been in vain. Then unexpectedly, the House passed a resolution awarding him $6,000. In the Senate Austin F. Pike of New Hampshire steered the measure through that body.[23]

After years of struggle Davis finally received one tenth of what he thought his country owed him for the destruction of his San Diego property. Only a few hundred dollars were left him after lawyer's fees, loans, and claims due to others had been paid. He had won only a Pyrrhic victory. But the San Diego adventure was finally over.[24]

[23]*Congressional Record*, 48th Cong., 2d sess. (Washington, 1885), pp. 505, 1279, 2482; *Senate Report No. 955*, 48th Cong., 2d sess. (Washington, 1885), pp. 1-3; *Senate Report No. 1151*, 48th Cong., 2d sess. (Washington, 1885), pp. 1-2. The latter document expressed concern over the previous testimony submitted which it called "very conflicting and of an unsatisfactory character." The Senate committee handling the Davis claim therefore recommended that $6,000, if not a much larger amount, ought to be allowed the claimant."

[24]About several of Davis's later visits to San Diego see San Diego *Union*, July 14, Nov. 25, 1869, Sept. 15, 1874, Mar. 18, Dec. 22, 1876 and Nov. 29, 1925. Details concerning his remaining financial interest in San Diego are in Davis to C. H. Forbes, Mar. 24, 1886 and Davis to H. H. De Voll, Mar. 21, Dec. 13, 1890, John Howell Collection. Hereafter cited as HC. See also Mrs. G. A. Pendleton to Davis, Apr. 28, 1892, SL, and Davis to Nellie D. Gleason, Sept. 7, 1896, HC.

CHAPTER IX

RANCHER AND FARMER OF THE
CONTRA-COSTA

EPRESSED BY HIS experiences in founding
American San Diego, Davis returned to San Francisco which
by now was far from a village of makeshift tents and temporary
structures. Very few streets, described in the Gold Rush days
as "Impassable, not even Jackassable!" remained. A miner returning to the new gaslit San Francisco after a year's absence wrote:

I really did not know where I was, did not recognize a single street,
and was perfectly at a loss to think of such an entire change. Where
I had left a crowded mass of low wooden huts and tents, I found a
city in a great part built of brick, houses, pretty stores.[1]

William Heath Davis and his generation had to make way for
something more than the mere transformation of adobe huts into
flapping canvas tents and again into baroque palaces at the once
quiet "village of mint." The Gold Rush which changed San
Francisco's physical form also ushered in a new set of merchants.
Davis missed the old familiar faces. In former times his chief
advantage had come from association with a closely knit group
of Yankee business pioneers and native Californians. Both groups
had now lost their early supremacy to invading easterners.

Davis doubted that he could make a successful commercial
comeback. Though still young compared to the scores of traders
who had recently invaded San Francisco, he learned that even

[1]Friedrich Gerstäcker, *Narrative of a Journey Round the World. Comprising
a winter-passage across the Andes to Chili; with a visit to the gold regions of
California and Australia, the South Sea islands, Java etc.* (New York, 1853), II,
45.

105

business methods had changed. The days when one could sell quantities of goods from a rude waterfront shed had passed and eastern capital had replaced the gold dust of forty-nine. Having strained his resources trying to found a new city in the south and suffering the enduring results of his losses in the fire of 1851,[2] Davis could muster neither the courage nor the capital to revive his business. Consequently he had to look elsewhere for sustenance.

Fortunately the lands of the Estudillos, dotted with clumps of oak and covered with matted grasses, needed attention. María's father, who had aged considerably, invited his son-in-law to join him in the management of the Estudillo domain. Rancho San Leandro seemed to offer the best hopes of regaining his faded fortunes and Davis appreciated his father-in-law's invitation.

One reason for the warm welcome given Davis was that he could help to solve a continuing problem in which an American voice would be most useful. A rivalry over a part of the ownership of the rancho marred José Joaquín Estudillo's relationship with his neighbors. Guillermo Castro, owner of the adjoining Rancho San Lorenzo, became Estudillo's chief antagonist in a controversy over the exact boundaries and water rights of their respective land grants.

Rancho San Leandro's history boasted a record of substantial achievement under the care of Don José, the first white man to settle beneath its sycamores and oaks. When that dignified settler initially claimed the area, bears could be trapped on the rancho's lands and remnants of an Indian tribe still lived there. The rancho covered an area about one league in size whose major boundaries were formed by the eastern shoreline of San Francisco Bay and by the willow and alder-lined banks of San Leandro and San Lorenzo creeks. Don José, who nursed a fondness for white cattle, stocked his domain with hundreds of snowy *vaquillas* which he could see at a great distance when he mounted the cupola of his ranch house. Although Estudillo's cattle mingled with the herds of his rival neighbors, he could easily distinguish his because of their white markings.

[2]Davis's property losses are noted in the San Francisco *Herald* and the San Francisco *Daily Evening Picayune*, May 15, 1851.

Don José died soon after his son-in-law joined him at San Leandro. Almost immediately Davis became the overseer of a large estate. The elder Estudillo's will not only gives the best contemporary description of Rancho San Leandro, but it also indicates the high degree of confidence which Don José had in his son-in-law. Although San Leandro's patriarch left the rancho's eight residences and half of its land and livestock to his widow, Doña Juana Estudillo, the remaining property went to their nine children, and Davis was named manager of the Estudillo estate:

I recommend my executor that when my son-in-law, Don Guillermo Davis, demands the number of two hundred cattle or five thousand dollars in silver, which I owe him as he shall choose to receive it, it be punctually paid to the satisfaction of all parties . . . from the common mass of the property previous to the division of the estate. I declare that I leave at different places on the Rancho three fields sown in Barley in company with Don Guillermo Davis. . . . [3]

Davis, his wife, and a growing family enjoyed San Leandro's surroundings. A faded brown photograph of the Estudillo home which Davis came to call his own shows a mansion fronted by steps leading up to a veranda that once surrounded it on three sides. This fourteen-room two-story structure was flanked by a shady garden replete with fruit trees and shrubbery. From its subterranean wine cellar came the many bottles of champagne for Davis's parties, which on one occasion cost as much as $1,500. These social events, pianoforte lessons for the children, and clothes from New York for his wife, characterized the mode of life adopted by the Davises in the great house.

Such gracious living was supported by a motley group of domestics over whom William Heath Davis himself reigned. The cook was one John Chinaman who produced dishes of "chow-chow" and curry which were said to have few rivals west of the Sierra. Though John was supposed to receive one dollar a day, his "conduct" sometimes left him little or no wages.

[3]Records, General Land Office, Board of Calif. Land Commissioners, Case No. 256 (San Leandro), "Record Copies of Evidence," XVII, 214-21, 288-90; "Record Copies of Petitions," II, 219-20; "Record Copies of Decisions," II, 514-15, Natural Resources Branch, National Archives, Washington, D.C.

One month when pay day rolled around, Davis charged him four dollars for a broken dish and twenty-two more for having "lost" some silver forks and a teaspoon. Another servant, a seventy-year-old Indian "houseboy" named Juan José, was indolent but, unlike his Chinese cohort, he would beg for a thrashing occasionally "to restore his energy and goodness," confessing that virtue was thereby whipped into him! These and several other workers loyally served the Davises, and they came to be regarded as a definite part of the family.

As part of his duties Davis assumed responsibility for the management of both San Leandro and that portion of a nearby rancho, called El Pinole, which his mother-in-law, Doña Juana, owned. In 1852 he made a good profit from his share of some 8,000 cattle and 1,000 horses stocked on that rancho. He deplored the fact that she was eventually tempted to sell El Pinole for only $38,000. Its purchaser would not have sold the rancho for $1,000,000, her son-in-law later stated.

The fortunes of Davis's first ranching years resulted indirectly from the Gold Rush which helped keep prices high for almost a decade. The increasing demand for beef had changed the nature of the industry—no longer were the carcasses of animals left to rot after being killed for their hides and tallow.

Since much of the finest grazing range and most of the largest ranchos were in southern California, northern cattlemen like Davis obtained much of their stock there, driving it north on the hoof. These drives were comparable in color and numbers of cattle herded with other better known American cattle drives.[4] Thousands of beasts were moved northward each year. Braving cattle thieves, Indian attacks, lack of water, stampedes, storms, and rustlers, the trail bosses and their *vaqueros* took weeks to complete one of these drives. In driving animals to San Leandro during the summer months special precautions had to be taken. In 1852 while Davis's men were herding almost 2,500 cattle homeward they were forced to make stops at ranchos along the way because of lack of water. At Rancho Los Ojitos they traded about 150 scrawny and bony beasts for 100 of

4Cleland, *Cattle*, pp. 103-104, 309, indicates the research possibilities of this subject.

Rancho Los Ojitos' fatter stock.[5] Upon arrival in the north the cattle were again fattened on the well-watered pastures of sheltered valleys. Independent cattlemen like Cave Johnson Couts of southern California's Rancho Guajome, who did not own northern grazing sites, rented pasture land at San Leandro from Davis in order to shelter their herds.[6]

Sometimes Davis himself would travel south to purchase stock and from Los Angeles he often reported his activities to María. In 1852 he wrote her of how he had recently bought from Don Emigdio Vejar some "seven hundred tame milch cows, many with suckling calves, and fifty head of cabestros [steers] for seven thousand dollars." After rebranding them, Davis drove the animals out of Los Angeles, along with another 700 steers bought for $13.00 a head.[7]

Among the southern suppliers of cattle were Juan Pablo Duarte, Eulogio de Célis, Loreto Amado, W. E. P. Hartnell, and Antonio María Lugo. From José Ramón Carrillo Davis often acquired horses, and from A. B. Thompson he obtained sheep from the channel islands. Davis bought livestock as far south as San Diego where José María Estudillo, a cousin of his wife's, had a stock ranch of some 5,000 cattle and several hundred horses.

To raise money with which to buy cattle Davis resorted to borrowing, to selling his remaining real estate in San Francisco, and to halfhearted attempts to collect old debts. Some of these accounts, dating from before the Gold Rush, might have been paid had he not allowed them to gather dust for so long in the drawers of his ranch house desk. The conclusion that his business operations were occasionally managed in an inefficient manner cannot be avoided. He seemed to be less and less discerning in overseeing vital business details.

His growing needs for new capital to modernize Rancho San Leandro became ever greater because of increasing competition.

[5]J. P. Duarte to Davis, May 27, June 9, 16, 1852, SL; J. R. Carrillo to Davis, June 4, July 6, 1852, SL.

[6]Couts to Davis, Apr. 7, 1852, SL.

[7]75 *Years*, p. 322; Vejar (sometimes spelled Vega and Bejar) to Davis, Dec. 6, 1851, and Davis to Vejar, Jan. 1, 1852, SL.

To grow such staples as wheat in profitable volume required a new and mechanized agriculture. Competing against those who had equipment such as horse-drawn plows and rakes which they had brought west posed a real problem for the California ranchero. As Davis became both a rancher and a farmer he needed money to buy corral fences, wheat threshers, and plows; he needed money to buy paint for the wooden farm buildings that were replacing crumbling adobes; bricks to line new wells, windmills, and barbed wire all cost a great deal. In addition Davis had to purchase not only cattle but also fruit trees for the orchards that he and others were planting on their lands. A sizable burden was also imposed upon him by the large number of ranch hands he had to feed in addition to the many mouths in his own family. To meet all these expenses Davis had to market numbers of cattle to large wholesale buyers such as the Pacific Mail Steamship Company. He also sent hundreds of bushels of barley and wheat to San Francisco in operations that were not unlike those of his Yerba Buena merchandising days.

These were busy and confusing years not only for Davis, but also for the society in which he lived. The historian of that California rawhide society, Robert Glass Cleland, has described the decades following the Gold Rush as the fusion of an out-moded and archaic agricultural system with an aggressive and sometimes ruthlessly expanding American frontier movement. The silver-trimmed saddles of the Californians stood in marked contrast to the steady depletion of their land. Increasing imports of superior eastern and Texas longhorn livestock caught rancheros like Davis with too many herds of stunted and overpriced cattle on hand. As pressing indebtedness fastened itself upon even successful rancheros, they ultimately had to sell half-grown colts in order to pay their debts. California's rancho economy was caught in a web of rising costs, diminished income, and heightened competition.[8]

Fatally timed with these difficulties, increasing numbers of Americans came to the Far West. Sometimes the newcomers engaged in rustling cattle, and ranchos like San Leandro, which

[8]Cleland, *Cattle*, pp. 107-11; Henry Chever to Davis, Mar. 10, 1850, SL.

possessed a water frontage, were especially exposed. The filchers who frequently came in schooners, landed on the rancho's banks at night and were sometimes assisted by the very *vaqueros* Davis employed to guard his herds—severe cattle losses resulted.

Added to the problem of thievery was that western phenomenon, "squatterism." After their arrival squatters challenged the right of California's rancheros to hold their land grants intact. One of the first of the families near San Leandro challenged was that of Vicente Peralta, who owned the most attractive sites along the eastern shoreline of San Francisco Bay. Davis had sensed that this area would one day support a larger population and had tried in vain, after the Gold Rush period, to purchase land from the Peraltas near Oakland where he wanted to found a town. He had implored them to allow him to develop their oak-covered slopes, prophesying that otherwise American squatters would seize this vulnerable region.

He did not exaggerate the danger for soon groups of land-hungry settlers squatted on the Peralta lands killing and freighting cattle almost nightly. Vicente Peralta once stumbled upon squatters loading some of his steers into their boats and was so outnumbered that he had to flee for his life. Unmanageable squatters, who formed small communities in the hills, stole at least $100,000 worth of Peralta cattle in a few months.

Had the Peralta family sold Davis its waterfront lands, he might have become the founder of the city of Oakland. Eventually a group of speculators took over the site for a pittance and the Peraltas were cheated out of a very large fortune. Years later Vicente Peralta admitted to Davis that he had been very foolish for not allowing him to develop this tract. It was, indeed, ironic that both San Diego and Oakland, which Davis had tried to found, became the successes of later speculators.[9]

Eventually squatters caused the Estudillos similar difficulties. Once land-hungry Americans reached California, they found

[9]Davis's plan for the development of a city at Oakland involved numerous prominent persons. See Agreement between Anthony Ten Eyck and Davis, July 27, 1849, UCLA. See also *History of Alameda County, including its Geology, Topography, Soil, and Productions* . . . (Oakland, 1883), pp. 325-27, 1000; The Peralta claim, challenged by the squatters, became a subject of wide discussion. See San Francisco *Daily California Chronicle*, Jan. 10, 1854.

that the bulk of the most arable land was in the hands of settled owners like the Estudillos. The available public domain promised them by various United States land laws was already occupied by California's ranchos. Perhaps all too naturally many of these rancho sites were destined to be pre-empted by predatory squatters.

The Land Ordinance of 1851 that rigidly challenged the validity of California's existing land titles helped the squatters. This law, which seriously affected Davis and most of his circle, was framed by a distant and poorly informed American Congress that had little realization of the severe pressure such legislation imposed upon California's native culture.

Here were two different land systems coming face to face. Had there been no gold rush, with its abnormal influx of easterners, the Anglo-American and Spanish land tenure systems in California might have been compatible. But Congress's pressured solution to this knotty problem—a board of land commissioners that rigorously sifted hundreds of land titles over a five-year period—proved extremely damaging to California's earliest residents. At great expense and inconvenience the confused natives, who had no knowledge either of American law or language, were required to uphold titles resting upon documents recognized for generations against squatter claims.[10]

The very fact that land titles could be challenged encouraged aggressive squatters to contest long established ownership. Cunning men were able to wrest land away from Californians like Davis's simplehearted in-laws and such conflict raised an unnecessary barrier between the two groups. It is no wonder that the sense of security that Californians had felt soon gave way to despair.

The story of the defense of Rancho San Leandro against squatters follows a familiar pattern. In 1852 the first newcomers settled on its rich bottom lands. To fortify their position they cleverly circulated a rumor that José Joaquín Estudillo had illegally enlarged his deed description. This inference was con-

[10]Cleland, *Cattle*, pp. 34-38, 102; see *Organization, Acts and Regulations of the United States Land Commissioners For California* (San Francisco, 1852).

venient ammunition for an assault upon the rancho's marginal lands. The banks of San Lorenzo Creek were soon so infested with shacks and tents that the area was called "Squattersville." It became a sizable task to protect the rancho from almost nightly acts of violence now that its boundaries were ringed by squatters and Davis for several years found it necessary to keep a gun strapped around his waist while outside the ranch house.

The troubles which Davis and his neighbors faced are illustrated by the activities of a squatter, Jacob Wright Harlan. When two nearby rancheros, Guillermo Castro and Barbara Soto, refused to lease Harlan some of their land near present-day Hayward, the squatter settled on Estudillo property along San Lorenzo Creek. Because this rivulet drained both Castro and Estudillo property and was still claimed by both families, Harlan and his fellow squatters asserted that it belonged to neither claimant. When Davis ordered him to cease building a shack and to leave the site, Harlan warned "that it was unsafe for him to meddle with the squatters." The intruder later boasted that Davis thereupon gave in and even

. . . asked what I would charge to plow for him 200 acres. . . . he immediately agreed to pay me that sum [$1,800] for the work and . . . told me that John R. Ward and one of Mr. Estudillo's daughters were about to be married. . . . and invited me to be present. . . .[11]

After completing the plowing, Harlan went back to what he considered his own land, which he later sold at a large profit.

Davis yielded to the squatters because law enforcement was not then well organized; an influx of frontier "bad men" made rural areas dangerous. When the invaders threatened to call upon such outlaws for help, conditions at San Leandro became intolerable, and Davis was to regret his irresoluteness. Late in 1852, while he was in southern California, 4,000 rancho cattle were prevented from reaching water along San Lorenzo creek by a fence which the squatters erected. Fortunately they were persuaded to allow the cattle to drink at the creek once each day. Added to this ignominy, they continued to shoot at the rancho's

[11]*California '46 to '88* (San Francisco, 1896), pp. 175-77, 169, 182, 221-26.

cattle and horses; on one occasion a ranch hand was shot in the chest. When Davis retaliated by tearing down several squatter shacks, he received a court summons. A "war" with them was only narrowly averted. These were such violent times that women and children were cautioned to stay indoors.[12]

Though the *Californios* theoretically had recourse to the courts, the law was interpreted by squatter judges and squatter juries and often administered by squatter sheriffs. In order to fight such a combination, Davis spent over $200,000 for legal representation to protect the Estudillo land titles. By 1856, as everyone grew tired of wrangling over the property, Davis's lawyers hit upon a plan to bring the squatters to terms. By deeding an interest in Rancho San Leandro to Clement Boyreau, an alien, their case fell within the jurisdiction of the United States Circuit Court. After a trial of several weeks, Judges Ogden Hoffman and Hall McAllister rendered a verdict favorable to the new plaintiff, Boyreau, and thus to the Estudillos. This was followed by a "squatter compromise" allowing the squatters to buy land. Though such land sales eventually altered the unity of the rancho, this solution seemed the only way to handle uninvited and immovable guests.[13]

In the struggle the squatters seldom failed to take advantage of the quarrels between the Estudillos and their neighbors. Issuance of a final patent by the General Land Office, in Washington, D.C., to the Estudillos was long delayed by the squatter-induced eruption of the rivalry with the Castros. When a group of squatters, joined by Guillermo Castro and Francisco Peralta, ancient rivals of the Estudillos, assembled a massive brief against Davis in Washington, he was extremely angry. Their testimony, however, did not impress United States Attorney General Edward Bates who revoked the pending squatter claim. Next they appealed to the Supreme Court and Justice Stephen J. Field, in delivering that court's opinion during 1863, also dismissed the

[12]"The Sunshine and Shadows of San Leandro," Huntington MS. DA 2 (276); *75 Years*, pp. 237-38; Records, General Land Office, Board of California Land Commissioners, "Record Copies of Evidence," XXI, 439-42.

[13]Ibid., "Record Copies of Petitions," II, 247; "Record Copies of Decisions," II, 448-54; J. B. Ward to Davis, Dec. 27, 1852, SL; W. C. Blackwood to Davis & Ward, Dec. 28, 1853, SL.

squatters' case. The Estudillos were jubilant but much poorer when the news finally reached them.[14]

The struggle in California over land ownership in the fifties and sixties did not help the rural and urban economies to prosper; indeed a depression was not far off. The situation was aggravated still further by the failure in 1855 of various important San Francisco business firms. As money grew scarcer the insolvent rancheros became easy prey for free-lance, high-interest money-lenders. Davis, like so many rancheros who were becoming financially exhausted by their legal skirmishing with squatters, had been paying ruinous interest rates on loans. When he could borrow no further on his only collateral—land—friends suggested that he prevail on the "old lady," Doña Juana, the matriarch of San Leandro, to sell more land to the squatters. The sales brought temporary financial relief. And with these funds Davis typically launched a new project. He still could not resist the temptation to speculate upon the future.

Despite his disappointments at San Diego and Oakland he embarked on a third adventure in town founding, this time at San Leandro. To take advantage of the pressure of an invading population, Davis and his new brother-in-law, John R. Ward, carved up part of Rancho San Leandro near the Estudillo mansion where a small community had already clustered. After Doña Juana deeded 200 acres of land for their townsite, they built numerous frame stores and even constructed a hotel, long known as the "Estudillo," at the corner of Davis and Washington streets. From it they built a plank road to a bayshore wharf at the Embarcadero de San Lorenzo.

In addition to leasing their town buildings, Davis and Ward continued, until the mid-fifties, to be the successful managers of Rancho San Leandro. Their land rentals for 1856-57 averaged $40,000 per year. In his *Seventy-Five Years* Davis claimed to

[14]U.S. Supreme Court, *Cases Argued and Adjudged in the Supreme Court of the United States*, LXVIII (Washington, 1864), 710-21; Brief in U.S. Supreme Court Library is *The United States Appelants vs. José Joaquín Estudillo; Appeal From the District Court U.S. For the Northern District of California: Supreme Court of the United States, San Leandro* (Washington, 1863); Calif. Private Land Claims Records, "Case No. 279," National Resources Branch, National Archives, Washington, D.C.

have "left the estate with more money due from the sales of land, than the rancho was owing for our costly lawsuits," and he asserted that the income from the ranch "was enough for two, yea, three Estudillo families."

Had the income from this "best and richest soil under the canopy of Heaven" been his alone, Davis might have answered letters from his old partner, Hiram Grimes, who begged for aid. Hiram's voice seemed to come out of a past that he and Davis no longer shared. In 1857 he wrote Davis that if he could not obtain aid "before 90 days, starvation will stare me in the face" and reminded him, "I assisted you to start in the world."[15] Davis would not endorse accounts due Grimes from the Frémont expedition and similarly refused to testify to his ownership of certain California properties. Davis may have been seeking revenge since he had never had a soft spot in his heart for Hiram Grimes, but it is more likely that, as sometimes happened, Davis was moved by those nearest him.[16]

As a matter of fact Davis made an effort to keep in touch with some of his old friends. He made frequent trips to San Francisco to visit them and often entertained them at San Leandro. On one of his jaunts across the bay he ran into John Sutter whom he had not seen for years. The faultlessly attired Swiss, who still owned part of his miniature kingdom "New Helvetia," suggested that they adjourn to the back room of Barry and Patten's hostelry to share a drink together. Over bottles of chilled Heidseick the two reminisced for several hours and relived such events as their 1839 trip up the Sacramento. As if eager not to break the spell, both were careful not to mention their early squabbles over money. Despite Sutter's self-praise, his company kindled a satisfying glow in Davis. To him Sutter was one of the symbols of old California and he felt that the story of the pioneers should be preserved. He vowed to write down for posterity some of the events Sutter had recalled to his mind.

[15]Grimes to Davis, May 20, 1857, UCLA.

[16]Ibid., Jan. 20, 1858; Grimes to Davis, Sept. 18, 1851, Apr. 18, 1853, Jan. 1, 1856, Apr. 6, 1857, SL and Oct. 6, 1859, UCLA; Davis to P. Peterson, Apr. 9, 1896, HC.

116

When old friends rode out to San Leandro to see Davis, they found him almost prodigal in entertaining them. Though he had turned his back on Hiram Grimes, he was generous to a former employee, Eli Southward, who lived at San Leandro for years as Davis's guest. James C. Pelton, San Francisco's first schoolmaster, also joined him there and wrote of his visit: "San Leandro was a new world to us, nature and humanity were enchanting and unique; and everything we saw and admired was 'de usted' (it is yours')."[17]

Life at San Leandro still exalted carefree living. Fiestas, *bailes*, and games helped mask the declining position of land owners like Doña Juana who were selling their land in order to continue their accustomed way of life. Above all these other activities her favorite rancho sport, like her son-in-law's, was horse racing. Rancheros were often horse fanciers and Davis was always eager to show off his stable by organizing races.

On one occasion a stranger named F. S. Humphrey boasted that his sleek mare, Sarah, could outrun any piece of horseflesh in the state. Davis defiantly invited him to run the mare against his horse, Yankee. Each owner, in a written agreement, promised to risk $1,000 and twenty head of cattle as a sweepstake prize. People from miles around lined the 400 yards of dusty lane down which the race was to be run and after the cry "Santiago!" the San Leandrans cheered their favorite on to victory. Yankee's triumph was marred for Davis when he discovered he had bet with a swindler who could not pay his wager. Much to his chagrin he learned from a friend, the well-known artist Edward Vischer, that Humphrey had already swindled him out of $5,000. In fact, Vischer called Humphrey "the Bigest scoundrel on the Earth." Davis eventually discovered that Humphrey did not even own the mare which he had turned over to him![18]

There was a real contrast between the cries of the spectators at this last big horse race at San Leandro and the steadily worsening economic situation in which Davis found himself. A high standard of living and a number of dependents in addition to

[17]*Sunbeams*, p. 229 and "Sunshine and Shadows."

[18]Davis and Humphrey, Agreement, dated Oct. 20, 1853, SL; Edward Vischer to Davis, Dec. 31, 1854, SL; W. B. Rude to Davis, Jan. 5, 1854, SL.

117

his large family created a great financial burden. María had borne him thirteen children, some of whom had died. Many of San Leandro's servants lived at the ranch house as did the more important ranch hands and a female tutor—described as homely and from Arkansas—who received the same wages as the cook, "$30 per month plus room and wash." Added to all these outlays of money Davis had assumed responsibility for sending Nathan Spear's son, William, through college.

In 1857 Davis was forced to give up his gracious life at the Estudillo mansion. A dispute with Doña Juana and one of her sons led to his resigning the management of Rancho San Leandro. He was able fortunately to turn to ranching and farming some 200 acres of his wife's portion of the family lands. This lay in the direction of Oakland, west of the modern Donovan Ranch.

From 1857 to 1870 Davis made a living on the smaller tract of land but his fortunes were never great. During this later era Davis also managed what he once described to Abel Stearns as "a very fine stock ranch" on some 2,600 leased acres from the Rancho San Felipe. Although he spent more than fifteen years near what is today the Oakland Airport, the only trace of his tenure in the area is a highway running from San Leandro toward San Francisco Bay. It is named Davis Road.[19]

Davis carried on his new pursuits amidst great difficulty. On a series of stubborn hills he raised cattle, grain, and vegetables. Large numbers of grasshoppers, unusual aridity, and, finally, a series of floods in 1861-62 made these precarious years for farmers. An almost simultaneous contraction in the demand for cattle caused livestock to be sold once more for the meager value of their hides and horns. Five thousand animals were marketed at Santa Barbara in 1864 for only thirty-seven cents each. Abel Stearns's annual income fell to only $300 and Davis made even less.[20]

The man's finances were becoming a mass of contradictions.

[19]Davis to Stearns, Jan. 24, 1858, Stearns Collection, Huntington Library; Tax Bills and Receipts, Oct. 18, 1858, July 21, 1859, ibid.; Cecil Corwin to the author, Nov. 6, 1951; J. F. G. Smith to Davis, Nov. 27, 1854, SL; O. C. Pratt to Davis, Dec. 27, 1862, SL.

[20]Cleland, *Cattle*, pp. 117-37, 198-200; Pratt to Davis, Dec. 27, 1862, SL.

RANCHO SAN LEANDRO, ALAMEDA COUNTY

Occasionally economic pressures would abate and during such periods some of his earnings would be spent for such luxuries as "strawberry gin," or a vacation at the nearby White Sulphur Springs Hotel. At the same time Davis failed to repay loans to relatives who demanded their money and who, in turn, owed others. Endless debts caused him to resort to all kinds of activities to earn more money. At San Francisco he marketed meat, grains, vegetables, and livestock. From his corral he sold horses to the Central Railroad Company for service on the company's street lines in San Francisco. He also rented plow horses, surveyed property, and sold cordwood to passing steamers from a landing at Rancho Pinole.[21]

In spite of his efforts new bills replaced those which Davis could liquidate and the demands of his creditors continued. Sometimes he ignored attempts to obtain repayment much as a middle-aged matron ignores birthdays. One merchant's distrust of Davis led him to write on the bottom of an old shoe bill, after sending a constable along to collect, "If Mr. Davis tells you that he would come and settle with us, don't mind him, you just tell him that you have orders to collect the bill."

The insolvency of farmers like Davis was in many cases not their fault. Weakened by years of litigation with squatters, they lived through an era of agricultural depression and were plagued by a series of misfortunes. In addition to wrestling with a tough clay soil, droughts, floods, and locusts Davis encountered still another adversity serious enough to break the spirit of any man.

Disasters induced by weather can sometimes be endured, but there is no protection against the most damaging of all the acts of God, the earthquake. In 1868 an earthquake struck northern California causing so much desruction that Davis and his wife determined to leave their portion of San Leandro forever. A description of their sufferings, printed in the pages of San Leandro's newspaper, the *Bulletin*, indicates that every building on his ranch was either damaged or destroyed. It read,

[21]White Sulphur Warm Springs Hotel bill, Aug. 30, 1861, and bill of P. A. Roach, wine dealer, Nov. 9, 1861, UCLA; Catarina Martínez to Davis, Dec. 27, 1862, Oct. 12, 1863, UCLA, and Feb. 3, 1861, SL.

His house was literally twisted in pieces and prostrated to the ground but the family escaped as if by a miracle. Mrs. Davis was caught in the ruins. She was badly but not dangerously wounded about the head and face, and is recovering from her injuries.

Davis could see no end to his troubles. From Hawaii came news that Robert's health was failing and although the two brothers were no longer as close as they had once been, William was greatly disturbed. He was proud of his brother's success in recent years. Robert had enjoyed a spectacular political career following his unsatisfying earlier life. His later achievements culminated in appointment to the Hawaiian Supreme Court and then to the lieutenant governorship of Oahu. Unfortunately, after the death of his wife, Robert seems to have tried to drown his loneliness in drink.[22] William, thinking that he might never see his only brother again, decided in 1871 to make a trip to Hawaii despite his insolvency. At the islands the two had a happy reunion, and William thoroughly enjoyed his escape from the drudgery of farming and the vexatious realities on the mainland. He was able to combine business with pleasure and sold some of the remaining parcels of family land on the islands.

Best of all, he unburdened himself to his brother and sought the older man's advice about the future. He told Robert of his and María's experiences in the earthquake and of their recent unwise investment in onions during a season when that crop was dirt cheap. William also described the fickle adobe soil which so often flaked into unworkable particles and caused the crops to fail. After hearing about the many difficulties, Robert advised him to get rid of the ranch and William wrote María to arrange for its sale.[23]

If the Davises had not sold the ranch they would have joined their heavily mortgaged neighbors whose farms were already under attachment by the sheriff. A new and oppressive California property tax made it steadily harder for these small

[22]Davis to R. G. Davis, Sept. 9, 1852 and R. G. Davis to Davis, Feb. 13, Mar. 18, 1855, Sept. 6, 1860, UCLA; Davis to Jones, Oct. 10, 1900, HC.

[23]Interview with Cecil Corwin, June 6, 1950; W. H. Spear to Davis, Feb. 14, 1871, UCLA; 75 Years, p. 202.

farmers to stave off foreclosure at a time when they were mort-
gaging their crops to secure temporary advances of money for
seed, machinery, and foodstuffs. This process was being repeated
throughout the United States as agricultural prices dropped
after the Civil War.

After selling their land Davis and his family moved to nearby
Oakland where he and María were forced late in life to cope
with new difficulties. She now had to learn how to rear a large
family in a city environment and her increasingly irresolute
husband had to seek a new occupation after twenty years of
ranching and farming.

CHAPTER X

THE DISCOMFITING SEVENTIES AND
EIGHTIES

URING THE DEPRESSION years that
followed his departure from Rancho San Leandro Davis could
not find suitable employment at Oakland and his plight reflected
general economic conditions in California. Now that the state
was tied to the nation by steel rails and the telegraph, news of
eastern financial scares, such as the Panic of 1873, quickly spread
from Wall Street; this event blackened California's financial
skies. The depression that followed resulted in numerous San
Francisco bank failures and a greatly decreased circulation of
money and investments. Added to this were other factors which
seemed timed to produce financial disaster: the exhaustion of the
Nevada Comstock mining lode, a failure of California's wheat
crop after several dry seasons, a dwindling livestock supply, and
an urban migration of the unemployed. At the same time that
Davis was seeking to create a second future for himself, bread
lines were becoming as common in California as in New York.
He had come into competition with the runaway sailors, street
thieves, and hoboes with blankets on their backs who now
crowded the California labor market.[1]

Amid trying circumstances Davis tried his best to hold a large
family together in the new city of Oakland overlooking San
Francisco Bay. When the family moved from the ranch, the
eldest son, Albert, was already an adult; Lilly and George were

[1]See John Philip Young, *San Francisco, A History of the Pacific Coast Metropolis* (San Francisco, 1912), II, 512 and Allan Nevins, *The Emergence of Modern America, 1865-1878* (New York, 1935), pp. 290-298 for a discussion of the national financial troubles of the seventies.

almost of age and other children ranged in age from 10 to 19. Soon after the move Willie, the youngest child and his father's favorite, was killed by a fall from a horse. The boy's death came at a time when disillusionment engulfed Davis, and this tragedy climaxed a feeling that fate had lately treated him most unfairly.[2]

Every member of the family was compelled to contribute to the support of their home. Two of the older children, Juanita and Anita, gave Spanish lessons, having become fluent in the language by conversation with their mother. Lilly and George joined their father in selling insurance. In addition to this activity, which he did not enjoy, Davis tried various other means of making a livelihood including selling real estate, appraising property, and translating documents.

Because of his lack of funds he could no longer associate with the level of society to which he had once been accustomed. Though still listed as a charter member of the Society of California Pioneers, his fame as one of California's earliest foreign settlers suffered an eclipse. Men who achieved success much later than Davis now received the public fanfare he craved. His former clerk Josiah Belden, for example, had become San Jose's mayor and rated a full-length biography in Oscar Shuck's *Sketches of Leading and Representative Men of San Francisco*. It galled Davis to note how the wealthy Belden joined the company of such notables as James D. Phelan, William C. Ralston, and James Lick on the pages of a contemporary "Who's Who." Davis knew that these men, whose lithographed resemblances glared at him out of such pretentious histories, were seldom even the West's "near greats" but only her "paying greats." He was disappointed that his past reputation did not earn a vignette.

As he failed throughout the 1870's to come to grips with his predicament, some of his most critical faculties seemed to slip away from him. In his youth Davis gave everyone the impression that he was a strong man. His remarkable business acumen had been combined with a resilient personal ambition which, when

[2]San Francisco *Alta California*, May 4, 1875; Davis to Archbishop Joseph A. Alemany, Oct. 14, 1875, UCLA; Cecil Corwin to author, July 15, 1950, Nov. 6, 1951.

matched by a natural alertness and native intelligence, had undoubtedly accounted for much of his early success. But now, as Davis continued to suffer the buffetings of misfortune, many of his most admirable qualities seemed lost to him. His early power of concentration, and an equally important determination to surmount adversity, had begun to deteriorate even during the ranching years. A once obvious frugality, attention to detail, and intuitive distrust of persons who might be harmful were traits replaced by a visionary and unstable optimism character-istic of his Hawaiian mother. As he aged Davis became unwisely sanguine over the outcome of too many ventures which had little or no chance of success. His tendency to exaggerate the workability of various plans undertaken late in life was prob-ably due, in part, to the great success achieved in his early years.

His personality and outlook were, of course, also greatly affected by his wife's family. He had grown to appreciate too deeply perhaps their native love of music, gay festivities, and enjoyment of the moment. Davis had never been a Sybarite, but now he sometimes allowed his tastes for good wine and the music of the guitar to crowd out pressing obligations.

Most of the circle of insolvent pre-pioneer settlers in Califor-nia to which Davis belonged had become observers of history rather than prime movers in it. This was disquietingly evident with Sam Brannan, Hiram Grimes, and even Thomas Oliver Larkin, who died much earlier than Davis; rarely did their original talents seem to carry over into the California of a later day. An added handicap from which Davis suffered particularly during the gloomy seventies was his inability to find a single occupation upon which to depend. He had been engaged in activities of many kinds and this tended to create an amorphous pattern of life.

In Oakland the pattern did not change. Davis continued to divide his time among numerous activities in an attempt to earn a livelihood. Property disputes were still a fruitful source of litigation in California, and he frequently testified in cases involving the early boundaries of land-grant ranchos and town sites; he became a recognized authority on land titles. To his fees for this service he added the money from occasional sales of the remaining odd parcels of his once extensive real estate holdings and commissions received from selling rancho properties for others. His services were also utilized by the Estudillo family's attorney, James D. Phelan (later San Francisco's prominent reform mayor), in the preparation of various Estudillo claims against the state. As he now had only a minor voice in the family's counsels, such assistance as Davis rendered the Estudillos these days was mostly a labor of sentiment.[3]

He needed every dollar that he could raise to care for himself and his family. The means by which he obtained money were secondary. Grasping at any reed in an attempt to pull himself out of his financial quagmire, Davis even brought suit against the prominent Hawaiian landholder Charles Brewer for several parcels of valuable Honolulu property left him by his brother who had recently died. The ill-advised litigation was ultimately decided against Davis by the Hawaiian Supreme Court.[4]

Growing indebtedness suggested to Davis that conditions beyond his control, or even that of his generation, seemed to be shaping the lives of men. The seventies and eighties were periods of social unrest in the Far West, an unrest which was reflected in the lives of other pioneers in similar straits. In California this was an era when the reformer Henry George decried the fact that small farmers like Davis had been driven off their lands because they could not compete with large absentee landlords who used migrant labor to till their huge farms.

In that age of agricultural discontent, of Grangerism, and then of Populism, Davis did not protest so vigorously as most critics against the railroads, California's most obvious targets for abuse. Instead of holding "the Octopus" responsible for society's major troubles, Davis condemned other "menaces." He was

[3]J. G. Estudillo to Davis, July 18, 1863, UCLA; J. M. Estudillo to Davis, Aug. 13, Sept. 21, Nov. 18, June 17, 1878, Nov. 25, 1879, UCLA, and Oct. 2, 1878, June 9, 1879, SL; Davis to J. R. Estudillo, Feb. 18, 1880, SL.

[4]William's last link with his Hawaiian background was broken in 1872 with his brother's death. A most complimentary eulogy of Robert was printed in the Honolulu *Friend*, Apr. 1, 1872. Regarding the Hawaiian lawsuit see *Equity of Petition to the Honorable Elisha H. Allen Chief Justice of the Supreme Court with Appendices* (Honolulu, 1857); *Appeal of William H. Davis vs. Charles Brewer to Supreme Court In Banco* (Honolulu, 1872), UCLA.

perturbed by the Oriental question that received so much public attention in the decade 1870-80. Like many other Californians, Davis thought that part of his difficulty was rooted in the Chinese infiltration of the labor market. Because he also believed that altogether too many people had come into California, he joined Denis Kearney's Workingmen's Party in its support of the slogan, "The Chinese must go!" He considered the "yellow peril" a threat to the laboring man.[5]

Although Davis attacked these "Celestials" as demoralizing heathens he was most sensitive to racial matters on which he himself was vulnerable. His nickname "Kanaka Davis" had long caused him discomfort. Also, his marriage had associated him with a national group that was fast becoming a minority. The declining social position of his immediate family led Davis to defend mixed-blood marriages and he often stated that superior children resulted from the "inter-marriage of the foreigners of early times with the Californians. . . ." He was careful to differentiate between Mexicans and the "superior" Californians. That ladies of these two groups were dissimilar he "proved" by noting how they even smoked their *cigaritos* differently!

It was natural that Davis should look back upon California's Arcadian past as a Utopia. He had won the respect of its people, and they had rewarded him with early success. Now that his once imposing social position had vanished, he missed those distant years. Davis wrote many letters to his friends in which he glorified the past. He frequently lamented to those who had left the Golden State that her slumbering beauty had been jarred by the dawn of a mechanized era that erased the grace from daily living. This new environment, he felt, tended to sharpen the antagonism between capital and labor.

As Davis aged, he also missed the comforts to which he was once accustomed. He possessed what his own generation would have called "high tastes." Though his children provided an increasing share of their own income, he still had relatively little money to spend on himself, and he craved more than just the "creature comforts." He was not content to smoke rancid pipe

[5] *75 Years*, pp. 379-81.

tobacco or to walk down the street in a sweat-stained frock coat. On the contrary, Davis required the luxuries of dress, smoke, and drink which befitted a man of position. With hand-rolled cigars selling at $4 a fifty, and tailor-made shirts costing $2 each, he had to scurry to keep himself outfitted to say nothing of his wife and family. And that was where his frustration sometimes arose.

By the late eighties his children noticed that their father left Oakland more frequently to cross the bay to San Francisco. It was also obvious to them that his mind was fastened upon other matters than his business. He seemed edgy and nervous whenever he discussed the routine of his insurance agency or his real estate sales at the family dinner table. As if to relieve his boredom he mentioned to many people how refreshing it was to go over to the "Golden Gate." He described how he felt a sort of inspiration whenever he approached San Francisco on the ferry. Often when it docked at the waterfront he knew so well, hundreds of gulls would dart across the boat's prow flashing their wings in the sun and soaring above the tall buildings just as they had done when the streets below were only bare and shifting sand dunes. Although old Candelario Miramontes' potato patch had long been Portsmouth Square and the city's muddy—indeed bottomless—main thoroughfare, Market Street, had become a wide boulevard, the flavor of the city had not been lost to Davis.[6]

He longed for the time and money to ponder and record the world of contrasts that separated San Francisco, and California generally, from frontier crudities. When his family found him scribbling historical notes on the backs of old envelopes, they realized that they must somehow help him to to escape the monotony of the real estate and insurance activities in which he had been only minimally successful. María and the children felt that he deserved a somewhat fuller life, even if they remained behind in Oakland. But, as he explained to them, he must find some sort of financial backing if he was to commence the one activity which he most craved—the writing of his memoirs.

[6]Davis to O. S. Cressy, Aug. 9, 1897, HC, is but one of many letters which typify Davis's thoughts about such subjects as politics, religion, and society in general.

Davis searched for several years before he found adequate financial backing to begin his "literary career." Fortunately he interested the two influential San Francisco publishers of the *Call* and *Bulletin*, Loring Pickering and George K. Fitch, in providing the financial support he needed to discharge his family responsibilities and to begin his writings.

With his finances arranged, Davis temporarily left his Oakland home to live in San Francisco where he said he could concentrate best. The city by the Golden Gate—like himself—had matured since he first knew it in 1831. But it had become a famous city while he had become an almost unknown figure in the later development of the hamlet which he had helped found. Indeed, Davis differed as much from the generation that now inhabited the metropolis as a California mission differed from a skyscraper. Still, the city was more like home to him than any other place on earth. He appreciated her new face and, as always, he savored the salty tang of San Francisco's incomparable atmosphere.

CHAPTER XI

WRITING YEARS

URROUNDED AGAIN by San Francisco's mists and by her increased commotion Davis, given to recollection in his autumn years, was bound to reminisce at length about California's past. Stored inside a massive and graying head were indelible memories of battling wind and spray before the mast, of poking into forbidden ports to smuggle and poach,[1] of hectic business activity during the Gold Rush years, of abortive attempts to found San Diego, and of later experiences as a California ranchero. After some of his old San Francisco friends became convinced that Davis should record his memoirs permanently, getting these recollections on paper became a matter of high priority to him.[2]

Davis had first tried another form of writing almost a half century before he commenced his historical work. Under the initials "W.H.D." he had, during the fifties, kept James Hutchings's *Illustrated Monthly Magazine* supplied with verse that was all too typical of an era of high-flown poetry. A poem entitled "Think of Me" had preceded "Home" and a most puzzling piece called "To Ella in New York." Still another contribution, "Song," had proved to be Davis's swan song, for the magazine thereafter ceased to print his writings.[3]

His later historical craftsmanship was of better quality than

[1]See Davis's "First Voyage of the Euphemia and Her Evasion of Revenue," Huntington MS. DA 2 (III), which deals with early smuggling activities.

[2]The historian Charles E. Chapman described Davis's mind as "exceptionally retentive" and overflowing with "important information which Hubert Howe Bancroft lacked."

[3]*Hutchings' Illustrated California Magazine*, I (1856-57), 127, 265-66, 272, 362, 368, 380, 381, 458, 504, 517; II (1857-58), 109-10, 167-68, 214-16, 265-66, 303, 317-19, 408-409, 469-71, 545.

his poetry and, by the late eighties, his articles began to appear in the San Francisco *Call*, the *Bulletin*, and the *Chronicle*. Newspapermen, including Pickering and Fitch, paid him only small sums for these pieces, but by rewarding Davis materially they encouraged him intellectually. Those sketches eventually formed the basis of his *Sixty Years in California*.

Another foundation for that book was the long manuscript entitled "Glimpses of the Past," which Davis was paid to compose for Hubert Howe Bancroft, producer of the first authoritative history of California. Of Davis's work one of Bancroft's numerous scribes wrote the editor of *The Century Magazine* describing the Davis of that day and also attesting to the regard in which he was held by those who were then piecing together the history of the Far West:

Though not an educated man, he had excellent powers of description, and a marvelous memory of little incidents and details of events which most men would have forgotten in a much briefer time. His narrations had reached some hundreds of pages at the time I left California in 1881, and were not completed at the time. Bancroft was much pleased by them. . . . He expressed his desire to me several times to make a book of it at some future time; and Mr. B[ancroft] did not discourage him in this idea. He was then poor, but had great expectation on account of some property in San Diego.[4]

When *Century*'s editor, attracted by this description, asked Bancroft's permission to use Davis's recollections nationally, a principal assistant of Bancroft's, Henry L. Oak, refused to release any of the Davis material for publication. Davis thereby lost the best chance he ever had to attract national attention to the long life of a pioneer.[5] He eventually tired of dictating recollections for Bancroft, with an occasional twenty dollar gold piece as a reward, and he began to prepare a history of his own. It proved to be but a short step to write out in long hand the

[4]Rufus Leighton to R. U. Johnson, Apr. 19, 1889, Robert Underwood Johnson Papers, BL.

[5]Oak to Leighton, May 10, 1889, UCLA. Davis's daughter Lilly remembered that her father dictated reminiscences to Bancroft for an occasional gold piece; interview, June 6, 1950, with the late Cora Clough, of Hayward, Calif., who knew Davis before he died, revealed a similar memory as did Cecil Corwin to the author, Nov. 6, 1951.

oral reminiscences which Bancroft had rated as the most valuable of all those submitted by the many pioneers he had interviewed.[6]

Davis was conscious of the fact that a writer was needed who had actually seen California's agricultural society displaced by urbanization. His challenge lay in portraying both the earlier society of California, symbolized by the squeaking two-wheeled *carreta* on her El Camino Real, and the new society exemplified by the railroad now on that same route.

After he pulled his first narrative together Davis, without difficulty, found a publisher, A. J. Leary. Much to his pleasure, *Sixty Years in California* met with the favor of the press upon its appearance. The San Francisco *Chronicle* reported that it had "few equals" in the "richness of its store of anecdote and reminiscence. . . ." Both the *Chronicle* and *Bulletin* pointed out, however, one of its most glaring defects—the book's lack of "plan and continuity." Although his digressions were innumerable, they were made with what newspapermen called "charming abandon" and most critics agreed that his writing possessed "an engaging simplicity of style" which they found "exceedingly enjoyable."[7]

The book drew some of its authority from the author's own manuscript collection. Davis was, in fact, one of the few pioneers to gather personal records representative of the political and commercial circles in which he had moved. The San Francisco *Monitor* reminded its readers that, unlike certain other local historians, here was a man who had lived the history he wrote. Fortunately Davis was more interested in describing people and events than in talking about himself—a characteristic which has given his *Sixty Years* permanency. It was, indeed, the modest tone and straightforward style of the book that made it attractive, despite its shortcomings, to the *Overland Monthly*.[8]

[6]Bancroft, *California Pastoral*, pp. 789-90; Bancroft, *History*, I, 56, lists Davis's name before those of Baldridge, Belden, Bidwell, Bigler, Chiles, Forster, Murray, Nidever, Sutter, Warner, and Wilson.

[7]San Francisco *Bulletin*, June 1, 1889; San Francisco *Argonaut*, June 9, 1889; *Overland Monthly*, XIV (1889), 103-108; San Francisco *Chronicle*, May 26, 1889.

[8]An additional appraisal is in San Francisco *Record*, May 25, 1889; Davis's manuscripts are described in Bancroft, *History*, IV, 10; V, 678, 679, 681, 683 and *California Pastoral*, pp. 470-472, 751 ff., 789-90.

Davis was not only pleased but surprised and grateful to reap a harvest of enthusiastic reviews of his first book. San Francisco papers like the *Weekly Commercial Record* were, if anything, too eulogistic:

Little did he, then young in years, deem that when three score of summers would have bronzed his features, or their accompanying winters have left traces of their frosts upon his head, he would sit down to the task of writing the best, most complete and original history which has ever been penned of the great and renowned state of California.[9]

The Oakland *Enquirer*, which planned to publish portions of the volume, stated that "no one now living is more competent to give a resume of events in this State." Davis reprinted such comments in a pamphlet designed to push the sale of his book. He earned several thousand dollars from his *Sixty Years*. But there were other compensations as well.[10]

His work had attracted such attention that he received an invitation from the Society of California Pioneers which twenty years before had almost ignored him, to write *A Short History of California* for distribution to its membership. Newspapers, too, wanted more of his reminiscences. All this success led Davis to believe that the market might be ripe for another of his volumes, and he began to assemble what he came to call the "Great Manuscript." Its title was to equal his number of years' residence in California by the time the manuscript reached the presses. Those years were to total up almost unceasingly.

For more than twenty years Davis worked hard at his writing. Each evening, when the city had quieted down, he labored late to check the accuracy of pioneer sketches assembled after hours of interviewing early settlers. To help him recall the past Davis mounted on the walls of his study numerous photographs of pioneers who were no longer living. As the old man looked up from his desk he could see, by the light of a gas lamp, the figure of Captain Grimes; next along the line of pictures was his old

[9] June 6, 1889.

[10] San Francisco *Morning Call*, Aug. 13, 1889; Ira G. Hoitt to Davis, Dec. 19, 1889, Oakland *Enquirer*, Aug. 31, 1889. Davis reprinted all the notices in "Reviews of *Sixty Years in California*" (San Francisco, ca. 1890).

chief, Captain Paty; nearby was a daguerreotype from which peered Captain "Webfoot" Phelps; farther across the room Nathan Spear seemed to contribute his encouragement. These portraits of old friends helped to remind him that he must resist the temptation to doze on his roll-top desk when the pen grew heavy and the hour late.

The author awoke each morning with a determination to go forth upon what he believed to be a historic quest, making pleas for assistance wherever he went. At the state capitol building in 1893 someone helped him spirit a photographer into legislative chambers to snap a photo of a painting of former Governor Micheltorena to the left of the speaker's chair. After the state librarian gave him various duplicate volumes, Davis boasted, "wherever I went I was recognized. . . ." For him such a rediscovery was most rewarding.[11]

His recognition as a historian gave him an opportunity to serve his lifelong friends the Californians. On one of his research trips Davis visited Platon Vallejo, the son of General Vallejo, who asked him to write a history that would not be "a smearing document," but one that would redress "historical errors" committed against his people. Government census takers now listed the Vallejos as foreigners and Vallejo accused Bancroft of misunderstanding the Californians; he wanted Davis to bare their "true story." Davis assured him that he would present their case in his book. He pointed out that he too had come to feel left out of the American society which he had helped install.[12]

While Davis was engaged in portraying the historically "true California," other writers, who sensed the presence of a vogue had the same idea and literary competition began to stiffen. The nineties saw the appearance of a rash of articles about California in national journals, sometimes accompanied by Frederic Remington's pen-and-ink illustrations. These pieces acquainted easterners with the Far West at a time when interest was at a new height. But much of this writing was by journalists whose accounts, though more entertaining than those by Davis, lacked

[11]Huntington MS. DA 2 (205).

[12]Vallejo to Davis, June 8, 11, 28, 29, July 6, 9, 1893, SL.

the substance without which the writing of history becomes a hollow exercise. *The Century Magazine*, for example, would have been well advised to follow the suggestions sent its editor by Bancroft's assistant. This critic wanted *Century* to carry articles by early Californians like Davis rather than those by journalists or "johnny-come-lately 'forty-niners'":

I refer to the people who possessed and governed California prior to 1849, the owners of immense ranchos . . . who gave the names of . . . saints to the towns. . . . a simple, unaggressive, honest, hospitable, and handsome race. . . . If you are inclined to pursue this matter, Mr. Davis' MS would be a valuable aid. . . . Mr. Davis will be identified by any of the older San Franciscans as 'Kanaka Davis'. . . . a pecuniary offer might not be amiss. . . .[13]

Unfortunately for Davis his writings never appeared in *Century* or in the pages of any other national journal. While men like John Bidwell were parading their "pioneer experiences" before national audiences, scant notice was paid those pre-pioneers who came to California a decade or more earlier than most overland migrants. Over half a century had passed since Richard Henry Dana's *Two Years Before the Mast* had been printed. Alfred Robinson's *Life in California*, published forty years before, already seemed forgotten. Now Bidwell, who was never even on the coast before 1842, was considered an authority concerning California's pastoral life.[14]

When one compares Davis's writing to other similar books, its superiority is immediately obvious. John Henry Brown's *Reminiscences and Incidents of Early Days*, for example, has been called a "literary curiosity" that "deserves a place in the Golden Gate Museum." An equally cluttered volume was S. C. Upham's *Notes of a Voyage to California*. These followed a succession of poorly organized reminiscences by Americans in California who rushed into print earlier than the more cautious Davis.

[13]Leighton to Johnson, Apr. 19, 1889, BL.

[14]See such work as John Bidwell, "The First Emigrant Train to California," *The Century Magazine*, XLI (1890-91), 106-30 and his "Life in California Before the Gold Rush," ibid., 162-83; Guadalupe Vallejo, "Rancho and Mission Days In Alta California," ibid., 183-92; Charles Howard Shinn, "Pioneer Spanish Families In California," ibid., 377-89.

Paying slight attention to those who surpassed him in public acclaim, Davis settled himself ever more deeply into the quarters furnished by George Fitch and Loring Pickering. In return, Davis contributed articles to Fitch's newspaper and was often mentioned in its pages.[15] Davis was quite happy in his new surroundings even though the once-gilded Montgomery Block was now a building sheltering an assortment of panhandlers and harlots. At one time it housed the coast's famous Bank Exchange Saloon with its once fashionable Italian marble interior hung with expensive oils. Here the Comstock kings and such writers as Robert Louis Stevenson, George Sterling, Jack London, Rudyard Kipling, and Ambrose Bierce had at one time or another, like Davis, stood around the saloon's beer pumps.[16]

Listed in the San Francisco City Directory as "author" and "historian" Davis for years continued to write, in addition to his newspaper pieces, hundreds of penciled drafts on legal-sized yellow sheets. A veritable mass of letters, asking information of old-timers and business firms, were typed by a secretary employed with money furnished by Fitch (Pickering had withdrawn his help earlier). She also clipped colorful stories from early issues of California newspapers which Davis carefully filed away for future reference.[17]

With such abundant source materials at hand Davis developed a basic literary handicap, an inability to stop writing. He produced a manuscript which editors called a literary "monster." Davis was unwilling to pare down the equivalent of two volumes of 1,200 pages each. His answer to critics of its size was usually: "I love my manuscript, every paragraph of it."[18] Davis tried for

[15]San Francisco *Chronicle*, Mar. 31, June 20, 1897, Jan. 16, Mar. 8, Aug. 7, Sept. 11, 1898; O. P. Stidger, whose knowledge of the Montgomery Block stretches back over fifty years, states that Davis could not have paid more than $6.00 a month for Room 22 (now Room 222) in "The Block."

[16]At one time even Dr. Sun Yat-Sen was a tenant in the Montgomery Block. See Idwal Jones, "What 'the Old Block' Knew," *Westways*, XL (Sept. 1948), 16-17; Asbury, *Barbary Coast*, 213.

[17]In some of his writings Davis relied heavily upon these newspaper clippings, especially the most exciting ones. See the similarity between his "A Bear Story," Huntington MS. DA 2 (229) and the account of a bear hunt in the San Francisco *Chronicle*, Oct. 25, 1896.

[18]Davis to N. D. Gleason, Mar. 23, 1896, HC.

years to market this offspring and kept "pushing ahead" its publication date: 1897, "Three or four months more and the great
manuscript will probably be in the state of New York for publication"; 1898, "I labor early and late with my assistants to close
the manuscript, and February 1899 will see the end of my big
task"; 1900, "My great manuscript is all in typewriting and the
work is finished preparatory to the press." In 1903 Davis wrote
the San Francisco publishing house Bancroft & Company that
it was "simply a matter of time" until money to publish his
manuscript would appear. Meanwhile, he noted, "I am adding
to and preparing new matter for the history." By 1905 the
manuscript had become *Seventy-Four Years in California*; still he
clung to the belief that it would be published. But Davis had
lost his sense of time and the many delays cost him the loss of
his only remaining benefactor. He was at his wit's end when he
wrote to Fitch:

I expected to see you on the 4th of the month which was your
practice. I called at the office . . . and I can hardly realize that your
good work as the benefactor of my valuable manuscript has ceased.
. . . May I ask that you reconsider and continue your help for a
brief period.[19]

Fitch never reconsidered.

Eastern publishers, as well as those in the West, were dismayed
at the prospect of publishing a manuscript of two and a quarter
million words. A friend who had tried to market the narrative
in the East wrote: "Mr. Doubleday declined to discuss the manuscript when I told him its length."[20] Eventually Davis offered
to dedicate his "Great Manuscript" to whoever would sponsor
its publication. No one came forward.[21]

[19]Letter draft, Apr. 7, 1905, HC.

[20]Davis to Houghton Mifflin Co., Nov. 26, 28, 1896, to Peter Paul, Dec. 19,
1896, and Mar. 17, 31, Jan. 18, May 12, Aug. 30, 1897; Frank Seaman to Davis,
Dec. 11, 1905, HC, and Davis to Seaman, letter draft, Nov. 29, 1905, Huntington
MS. DA 269; O. S. Cressy to Davis, Oct. 10, 1896, HC.

[21]Cressy to Davis, Oct. 31, Nov. 11, 1896, and Davis to Cressy, Nov. 17, 1896,
HC; Davis to Mrs. C. B. Flannagan, June 10, 1905, HC; Percy T. Morgan to
Davis, Oct. 31, 1905, in author's possession; San Francisco *Chronicle*, June 20,
1897, and Jan. 16, May 6, 11, Aug. 7, Sept. 11, 1898.

Distressed because he was unable to market his work, Davis withdrew to his literary laboratory in the Montgomery Block. There physical comforts were few. Its only window opened on the back side of a steam heating plant whose sheet metal surfaces reflected the glare of the sun in the summer and intensified the monotonous patter of rain in the winter. He saw his children only when San Francisco Bay's chilling winds abated enough to make it comfortable for him to cross by ferry. Correspondence became his main diversion and occasionally his despair would be lightened by a satisfying note such as he once received from his competitor, John Bidwell: "Californians of whom we may ask information of men and events are becoming remarkable few. You are the only literary one of *ante bellum* and *ante aurum* times. . . ."[22]

This, Davis believed, was indeed a compliment to be cherished. Why could not the publishers also see the merit of his works? As if to escape from his preoccupation, Davis on occasion turned his attention to politics. Perhaps, to him, the most meaningful political event of his lifetime was the election of President McKinley in 1900. With Fitch he worked hard to help bring about a McKinley victory; Davis had even put aside the "Great Manuscript" for a time to work at Republican headquarters. He was so moved by his hatred of William Jennings Bryan and his "co-anarchists" that he wrote a friend:

If McKinley is favored with the result of the great national contest, I will push the history. . . . If on the other hand Bryan is elected I will deposit it in a fire proof vault and await events.[23]

Davis seemingly reasoned that the nation would stop reading if Bryan were elected.

This brief excursion into politics did not mask the fact that he was hurt by the lack of interest in his "Great Manuscript." He tried hard to arouse the attention of such prominent local personalities as Senator George Hearst's wife, Phoebe Apperson Hearst, and President Benjamin Ide Wheeler of the University

[22]Bidwell to Davis, Apr. 18, 1895, is printed in 75 *Years*, p. 158.
[23]Davis to Cressy, letter draft, Aug. 30, Sept. 7, 1896, Sept. 6, 1899, HC.

of California. Davis eventually resorted to selling portrait space in his contemplated volumes. About seventy descendants of early governors, statesmen, traders, and merchants purchased space first at $350 a page, then at reduced rates. Many people who sent Davis money expecting to see themselves in the volumes were incensed when their pictures were never published and Davis no longer had the funds to reimburse them.

Unfortunately Davis lived too early to attract the attention of a group of professional historians that ultimately came to the University of California after Hubert Howe Bancroft sold that institution his library. He did correspond briefly with two scholars, Professors C. L. Goodwin and George Davidson. Whenever they wrote to ask him about some historical fact, his replies were designed to attract them to his work. The motivation should have come from them. Here was an opportunity for historians to obtain a series of unparalleled first-hand accounts of California's historical past.

Not until long after his death did his writings receive the recognition Davis had thought they deserved. In 1929 his numerous manuscript fragments were compiled and published by John Howell under the title *Seventy-Five Years In California*.[24] Reviewers hailed the book as a welcome addition to western literature. Moreover praise of his writing has been continuous. Not only the historians, Hubert Howe Bancroft and Charles E. Chapman, but the pioneer author of *Early Days and Men of California*, W. F. Swasey, and California's only native philosopher, Josiah Royce, applauded Davis's writing. Robert Ernest Cowan, the bibliographer who helped bring out *Seventy-Five Years*, believed that the Davis "narrative of men and events of the period 1840-1850 is the most intimate and complete that we possess."[25] The Zamorano Club, composed of booklovers,

[24]G. H. Davis to Howell, June 21, 1926, and Howell to G. H. Davis, letter draft, June 23, 1926, HC.

[25]William F. Swasey, *The Early Days and Men of California* (Oakland, Calif., 1891); R. E. Cowan quoted from Glen Dawson, *Californiana; A Priced Catalogue of One Thousand Books and Pamphlets relating to the history of California* (Los Angeles, 1943), p. 40; Josiah Royce, *California from the Conquest in 1846 to the Second Vigilance Committee in San Francisco; a study in American character*, intro. by Robert Glass Cleland (New York, 1948), p. 31; Bancroft, *California Pastoral*, pp. 789-90.

still includes this book and *Sixty Years* in a list of "indispensable" California books. One connoisseur has recently stated: "No book written by a contemporary dealing with California has been so widely quoted. It is the acknowledged source book for the period which it covers."[26] The writer Phil Townsend Hanna, in a list of 3,000 titles essential to a proper understanding of California, rates the Davis volumes among the twenty-five works of "commanding interest."[27] The latest estimate of *Seventy-Five Years* comes from the pen of Franklin Walker:

There are . . . accounts from which the historian builds his mature estimate . . . or to which the lover of old journals turns for picturesque detail or amusing incident. Certainly such a one will not neglect William Heath Davis, *Seventy-Five Years In California*, in which that son of Hawaiian-Yankee merchants tells of his early visits to California from the Venice of the Pacific, or of the open smuggling of the island traders, or of the many incidents of rancho life which he saw. . . . Episodic and discursive, light-hearted and amiable, it supplements the more effective contemporaneous accounts found in Pattie, Dana, and Robinson.[28]

Today *Seventy-Five Years* has joined Davis's first book as rare Californiana. Writers have long mined both works for material to lend authenticity to often mediocre narratives. Dozens of popularizers, novelists, and amateur historians have culled information from both of his books. Their constant use justifies the years of struggle during which Davis dedicated so much energy for an almost unrewarded labor of love.

[26]Glen Dawson, *Southwest Books, a priced an indexed book catalogue* (Los Angeles, 1954), p. 28; *The Zamorano 80, A Selection of Distinguished California books made by members of the Zamorano Club* (Los Angeles, 1945), pp. 20-21.

[27]*Libros Californianos, or Five Feet of California Books* (Los Angeles, 1932), pp. 36-37, 43. See such other appraisals as R. L. Duffus in *The New York Times Book Review* (June 16, 1929); *California Arts & Architecture*, XXXV (1929), 39; *Touring Topics*, XXI (1929), 46; *Calif. Hist. Soc. Quarterly*, VIII (1929), 183-85.

[28]*A Literary History of Southern California* (Berkeley and Los Angeles, 1950), p. 37. Reprinted by permission of the author.

CHAPTER XII

PIONEER OF PIONEERS

IN 1906 DAVIS WAS eighty-four years old. He continued to work on the "Great Manuscript" and each night, long after the occupants of the Montgomery Block had gone home, his light shone through an open window on the second floor. The old man in a worn serge suit was usually bent in concentration over a roll-top desk. A gaunt, leathery face rose above a celluloid wing collar and a wide scarf-tie. On the night of April 17, after he had scanned the yellowing pages of the manuscript for several hours, he let his orange-colored fountain pen slip from his fingers and leaned back to rest before going to visit his family in Oakland. This was his last night of work in the Montgomery Block.

During the early morning hours of the next day the holocaust of the San Francisco earthquake twisted the city into a mass of rubble. For several days the city was in a state of confusion. Once the smoke from the great fire that followed the quake had cleared, Davis recrossed the bay and picked his way through a sea of wreckage to the Montgomery Building. But United States Marines stationed at the entrance prevented him from entering the condemned structure. When he finally was allowed into his office he found no manuscript. This proved to be the final tragedy in the life of William Heath Davis. Whether his writings were stolen by vandals or were somehow removed by the authorities who prevented Davis from entering the building, has never been explained.[1] The loss sapped him of his remaining energy. The aged man did not have the vigor to rewrite his

[1] *75 Years*, p. vii. The only person besides Davis who saw the tin dispatch boxes was Robert Ernest Cowan. See Douglas Watson to Cecil Corwin, letter draft, Mar. 13, 1930, HC. A tale, told the writer as recently as May 21, 1952, is that the lost Davis manuscripts were among a batch of 10,000 documents given Robert

many years of work.[2] A grandchild who was only eleven years old at the time of the earthquake and fire, and who could scarcely absorb the impact upon him, nevertheless recalled vividly his reaction forty-five years later and wrote: "I can see him coming up the street, and sinking down on the front steps in tears" because of his anguish over having just lost his "Great Manuscript."[3]

According to a friend, during one moment of revived enthusiasm, Davis did vow to rewrite his memoirs:

When I saw him at E. W. Howard's house in 1907 he was over eighty years, a typical New England type, thin and stooping. . . . to all of us there sitting on the lawn with his old black bag open and Templeton Crocker looking over the little memorandum books in it with great excitement. . . . Mr. Davis stood up and announced 'I am over 80 years old but dar gone it! I am going to have to put it together again!'[4]

But his energies drained and his finances at their lowest ebb, Davis never completed the promised rewriting of his work. As a result the bookdealer and bibliographer, Robert Ernest Cowan, acquired from him a rare "trunk full of old papers" which Davis had tried unsuccessfully to sell to others, including the California State Library. Cowan, who estimated their value for the reconstruction of California history to be unparalleled for the period covered, remarked that "they form the only body of commercial and mercantile correspondence extant."[5]

---

Ernest Cowan by his good friend Colonel George W. Granniss. Granniss was executor of the law firm of Halleck, Peachy & Billings and inheritor of many manuscripts left in the Montgomery Block's basement. The colonel had a reputation for "burning" documents, or at least for causing them to disappear. Whether some Davis material was mistakenly included among the Granniss papers, may never be known. See Harold D. Carew, "Arbiter Elegantarium In the Realm of California Books," Touring Topics, XXII (1930), 32-33.

[2] 75 Years, p. vii; letter to author from Cecil Corwin, Apr. 10, 1950.

[3] Alice Davis Riecker to author, May 1, 1951.

[4] Although Templeton Crocker, a friend and San Franciscan of prominence, was interested in Davis's notes, he, unlike Fitch earlier, made no offer to subsidize Davis and the latter gave up plans to rewrite his work. F. S. Whitwell to author, Sept. 13, 1950.

[5] Cowan to Margaret Eastmen, Mar. 13, 1911, SL; Cowan, "A Description of the Davis Papers, 1840-1852," SL; Davis to J. L. Gillis, Nov. 29, 1904, Jan. 12, 1905, SL.

The motif of these last years was obscurity, indeed, almost anonymity. Scarcely a newspaper story about Davis appeared now. The magazine *Out West*, in publishing his signed picture, still called the pioneer "probably the only 'American' yet alive" when California's first newspaper was published. This, however, was an article about a newspaper, not about Davis.[6] He came to feel increasingly that there is no sadness to match the loneliness of old age. His grown children had gone their separate ways and his wife, some years after the turn of the century, had entered the King's Daughters of California Home For Incurables.[7] All the old pioneers had died as Davis reached the end of his life. Fitch and Howard had been gone for a half century. Larkin too had been among the earliest to die. Stearns had followed him in 1871, Sutter in 1880, Leese in 1892, and Warner in 1895—still, they were deep within the memory of one who had outlived them all.

Divested of most old friends and in straitened circumstances Davis, soon after the fire, moved across the bay to Hayward to live with a married daughter, Anita. She had married a prominent journalist, Edwin Clough, who provided Davis with a separate dwelling to the rear of their home. He slept in this brown, shingled "go-down" limping into the main residence at mealtimes. The house, which Anita filled with Oriental *objets d'art* from her husband's travels, still stands but Davis left behind scarcely any possessions to mark his residence in it.

A grandchild remembers him as "a very impressive gentleman, with a great deal of reserve." She found him "always very serious," especially whenever he gathered the whole family around to give them counsel and she never felt as though she could "run and jump into his arms," as most grandchildren might.

His Hayward retreat served him well. He would hobble with a cane around the streets of the town or sit on a bench under Chinese elms watching people pass by and children at play. To those who stopped to chat he expressed an almost patriarchal

[6]W. J. Handy, "The First California Newspaper," *Out West*, XXIII (1905), 63; Davis to Mary Foreman, letter draft, July 28, 1905, HC.

[7]G. W. Caig to author, Feb. 10, 1951; Davis to Morgan, letter draft, July 1905, HC; Davis to Cressy, letter draft, Nov. 23, 1898, HC.

pride in the California he had known. This, in fact, was his main interest in those last quiet years.[8]

Davis eventually suffered a paralytic stroke which left him helpless physically but mentally alert. His daughter engaged a Syrian student at the University of California as houseboy and companion who, much to the invalid's gratification, listened to him for hours. Finally on Sunday, April 18, 1909, Davis's strength ebbed completely and he died, with his daughter and son-in-law at his bedside. The event caused no great stir, least of all in Hayward, and hardly more in nearby San Leandro and San Francisco.[9]

A pioneer of pioneers had died, but generations of Californians would continue to remember him for his writings and for his role in the development of the Pacific West.

[8]Interview with Cora Clough and Cecil Corwin, Hayward, Calif., June 6, 1950.

[9]San Francisco *Call*, Apr. 20, 1909; A MS obituary is in the Archives, Soc. of Calif. Pioneers, San Francisco, V, 117; *Grizzly Bear*, V (1909), 17.

143

# DESCRIPTIVE BIBLIOGRAPHY OF
# MANUSCRIPTS

No BIOGRAPHER could complain that the correspondence of William Heath Davis was not sufficiently comprehensive. There are Davis manuscript collections in many archival depositories which vary in importance, period of coverage, and completeness. In addition, Davis manuscripts are scattered among private collections and his letters continue to crop up from time to time. The following is an annotated listing of the principal Davis manuscript sources:

ARCHIVES OF HAWAII, HONOLULU, HAWAII.

The Francisco de Paula Marin Journal (1809-26) contains recollections about Captain Davis's Hawaiian years.

BAKER LIBRARY, HARVARD UNIVERSITY GRADUATE SCHOOL OF
BUSINESS ADMINISTRATION, CAMBRIDGE, MASSACHUSETTS.

The William Appleton & Company Papers (Dexter-Appleton Collection), of some 181 volumes and boxes, cover the California activities of that firm for the period after 1841. They include mention of Henry Teschemacher, Alfred Robinson, and other early Boston hide and tallow droghermen. Perhaps the finest holdings anywhere for the period before Appleton & Company commenced its California business is the Bryant, Sturgis & Company Collection which covers the period 1811-71. These records go beyond the period when the firm ceased its California business. The John Jacob Astor Collection contains some correspondence concerning the Alaskan fur-trading activities of Captain Davis, Sr. Included in the library's holdings are the Account Book of the ship *Eagle*, Eliphalet Davis, master, 1820-21, the records of Davis, Sr.'s partners in the firm of Bordman and Pope of Boston and ship journals of the *Loo Choo* and *Barnstable*.

Davis's correspondence at this library is scattered throughout the Mariano Guadalupe Vallejo, Thomas Oliver Larkin, and Henry Delano Fitch Collections. These are all strong for the period prior to 1850. The Nathan Spear Collection, Robert Underwood Johnson Papers, and George K. Fitch Collection also include items of importance for the earliest and latest periods of Davis's life. Among the Uncatalogued Manuscripts are to be found some rare Johann Augustus Sutter letters concerning Davis. See also the early (1833-36) "Nathan Spear Account and Letterbook." The Alviso and Pico manuscripts yielded some letters written in the period 1838-44. Although the Bancroft Library possesses no Davis Collection, its William Heath Davis Folder contains note "scraps" to sources used by the historian Hubert Howe Bancroft in preparing his "Pioneer Register" and other sections of his *History of California*. The Departmental State Papers (1821-46) consist of 20 volumes of manuscript transcripts from early official California archives. These and the Monterey Consulate Archives contain information about the early trading activities of both Davis and his father in California. Several individual memoirs of the Spanish period were of value: José Joaquín Estudillo's "Documentos para la historia de California" (1776-1850) is a basic manuscript reminiscence of the Estudillo family by Davis's father-in-law. Of similar vein is Antonio María Osio's "Historia de California." The only Davis literary manuscript at the Bancroft is his first. It is the important 296-page source written for H. H. Bancroft and entitled "Glimpses of the Past." The major manuscript source concerning Captain Davis is the "Solid Men of Boston In The Northwest" by Captain William Dane "Webfoot" Phelps. The manuscript log of Captain Davis's ship, the *Arab*, is also at the Bancroft Library.

HENRY F. BRUNING COLLECTION, PALO ALTO, CALIFORNIA.

Mr. Bruning has collected a variety of Davis manuscripts principally concerning his activities at the beginning of the conquest of California. Bruning also owns Davis's passport of 1841, signed by Governor Alvarado.

CALIFORNIA HISTORICAL SOCIETY, SAN FRANCISCO, CALIFORNIA.

The "William Heath Davis Letterbook (1844-1859)" contains letters by Geary, Larkin, Hyde, Folsom, Leidesdorff, Halleck, Mason, Stockton, Frémont, Howard, and Gwin. The Jacob P. Leese Collection parallels the period of Spear's Yerba Buena activity. The "Collection of Maps of Streets Proposed for San Francisco," attributed to Davis, tax receipts, checks, and bills pertaining to his San Francisco business are also in the Society's possession.

CALIFORNIA STATE LIBRARY, SACRAMENTO, CALIFORNIA.

This depository's William Heath Davis Collection is the most significant single source of Davis materials extant and one to which Davis himself contributed during his lifetime. It includes several thousand business notes, letters, and documents written principally to Davis from 1836 to 1909. The Davis "Letterbook" of this collection contains copies of about 100 letters written by him from 1846 to 1858. This "Letterbook" and all the correspondence of this collection from 1848 to 1896 has been microfilmed and is in the library of the University of California at Los Angeles. Robert Ernest Cowan, the bookseller and bibliographer, who sold the collection to the California State Library in 1911, called it the finest grouping of commercial and mercantile correspondence in existence for the period 1840-50. It includes correspondence of the principal Yerba Buena merchants of that period: Larkin, Leese, Vioget, Leidesdorff, Howard, Mellus, Green, Reading, Hensley, Scott, Boggs, Vallejo, Estudillo, Spence, Folsom, Brannan, Phelps, Bartlett, and Hyde; and it contains orders, bills, receipts, shipping papers, manifests, clearances, and business letters of commercial and military origin; business firms in the East and individuals in the principal trading centers of Hawaii, China, Latin America, and California, through the Gold Rush period especially, are also represented. The greatest strength of the collection, which totals several thousand manuscripts, is in the period prior to 1860.

ESSEX INSTITUTE, SALEM, MASSACHUSETTS.

The original log of the *Eagle* for various voyages from 1753 to 1836, unfortunately unrelated to Captain Davis's ownership of that vessel, is at the Institute. A large amount of extraneous naval materials are also available.

HOUGHTON LIBRARY, HARVARD UNIVERSITY, CAMBRIDGE, MASSACHUSETTS.

The James Hunnewell Papers contain some information concerning the relation of this well-known Boston merchant with Captain Davis. The Josiah Marshall Papers (1818-41) contain correspondence of the Boston firm of Marshall and Wildes and mention Captain Davis's and John Coffin Jones's business connections with Dixey Wildes and others.

JOHN HOWELL COLLECTION, SAN FRANCISCO, CALIFORNIA.

This collection contains many hundreds of pencil and typescript letter drafts written by Davis primarily between 1880 and 1906. These mainly concern his attempts to find a publisher for his long manuscript. They are, however, rich in his political and social observations as well as personal data. They mirror the social currents of the period to good advantage. Many incoming letters from his friends of long standing give the collection a personal flavor that enhances its value. A few unpublished literary manuscripts are in the collection.

HENRY E. HUNTINGTON LIBRARY, SAN MARINO, CALIFORNIA.

The William Heath Davis Collection contains few letters. More numerous are commercial documents, receipts, and memoranda, 237 pieces of which were acquired from the collection of A. S. Mac-Donald covering the period 1840-60. The remainder of the collection is an excellent accumulation of literary manuscripts, ephemera, and unpublished manuscripts perhaps 150 in number. The original manuscript of Davis's *Sixty Years in California* is here as are the only unpublished Davis literary and historical materials, aside from those in the collection of the San Francisco bookseller, John Howell. Most of this collection was purchased from Howell. The Huntington's Abel Stearns Collection contains a few Davis items. Its William A. Leidesdorff Collection features only occasional references to the activities of Davis.

KING-DAVIS GENEALOGY, HONOLULU, HAWAII.

The late Mr. William Heath Davis King, a great-nephew of Davis, compiled some unusual genealogical notes from data which has been in his family for many years. Original photos of his and Davis's forebears have increased the value of these notes, photostats of which are in the author's possession due to the kindness of Mr. King.

LOOMIS PAPERS, DETROIT, MICHIGAN.

The Elisha and Maria Loomis Diary and Papers are in the possession of Miss Albertine Loomis of Detroit, Michigan. Written by two missionaries they are rich in anecdotes concerning the activities of Captain Davis at Honolulu during the first years of the establishment of the American Board of Foreign Missions there.

MONTEREY CUSTOMS HOUSE, MONTEREY, CALIFORNIA.

The "Import Duty Record Book (1846-1862)" lists the dates of arrival, departure, and fees collected from Davis's various vessels.

NATURAL RESOURCES BRANCH, NATIONAL ARCHIVES, WASHINGTON, D.C.

The Records of the General Land Office, containing transcripts of the deliberations of the California Board of Land Commissioners after 1851, were invaluable in reconstructing the history of Rancho San Leandro when its title was in jeopardy. The Record Copies of Evidence, concerning evidences of ownership produced by Davis and the Estudillos are on file in the National Resources Branch as are the Petitions, Decisions, original *Expedientes* of Rancho San Leandro and many other California ranchos, and title information and court records, including correspondence concerning the Supreme Court decision regarding Rancho San Leandro.

PASADENA PUBLIC LIBRARY, PASADENA, CALIFORNIA.

The Letters of San Diego Pioneers (1850-55) at the Pasadena Public Library is a collection of about 100 letters concerning Davis's wharf construction activities at San Diego. Many details about the founding of New Town may be gleaned from these letters.

PEABODY MUSEUM, SALEM, MASSACHUSETTS.

Correspondence with this notable maritime library elicited information about several of Captain Davis's early vessels. It is a depository of real significance concerning New England shipping activities.

SAN DIEGO HISTORICAL SOCIETY, SAN DIEGO, CALIFORNIA.

The Historical Miscellanea Section of the society contains a Davis file as well as a file (Early San Diego Houses) that has information about Davis's construction activities. Data about such men as Miguel de Pedrorena, José Antonio Aguirre, A. B. Gray, Thomas Johns, and William Ferrell, who were Davis's San Diego partners, is in the society's Biographical File.

UNITED STATES DEPARTMENT OF STATE CONSULAR RECORDS AND MANUSCRIPTS, NATIONAL ARCHIVES, WASHINGTON, D.C.

Consular Records, Manila, Vol. I, contain dispatches from Andrew Steuart, Consul at Manila, to John Quincy Adams, Secretary of State, mentioning the early sailing activities of Captain Davis and his cohorts. Consular Records, Valparaiso, 1820, contain similar records. Consular Letters, Honolulu, Vol. I, include dispatches from Davis's stepfather, John Coffin Jones, to Secretary of State Adams during 1821 and to Secretary of State McLane during 1834. The records of the French spoliation claims revealed very detailed earlier correspondence regarding Jones.

Court records, correspondence, and original brief of the San Leandro Rancho squatter case are on file.

UNIVERSITY OF CALIFORNIA LIBRARY, LOS ANGELES, CALIFORNIA.

The William Heath Davis Collection, a section of the Cowan Collection, consists of several hundred representative letters from 1842 to 1882. Cash, account, and cargo books concerning Davis's various business houses and shipping interests are also included. The numerous bills and receipts are principally from the periods 1840 to 1850 and 1855 to 1870. Its main strength is in the period of Davis's founding of American San Diego. The Charles E. Pickett Papers, also in the Cowan Collection, include letters of the 1840's from Pickett regarding the management of Davis's Yerba Buena interests. They are printed in an appendix to Lawrence Clark Powell's *Philosopher Pickett* (Berkeley, 1942). Also in the library is a 550-page doctoral dissertation by the author entitled "Trading in Golden Lands: A Biography of William Heath Davis," which contains, in much detail, the story not only of the subject of this biography but also of his father's circle of trading colleagues in the Pacific.

# INDEX